Three Feet Under

JOURNAL OF A MIDLIFE CRISIS

By

Christee Gabour Atwood

BOOK
REPUBLIC

Book Republic Press
857 Broadway, 3rd floor
New York, NY 10003

Library of Congress Control Number 2005920426
ISBN 1-58042-179-2

Book Republic Press is an imprint of Cardoza Publishing

This book is dedicated to three incredible people.

David. By the end of this book, you'll understand why.

Ruth Bryan Gabour, my mom. If I were half the writer she is, this book would be a million-seller.

James Anthony Gabour, my dad. From the time he published my first elementary school newspaper, he's been my biggest fan ... and I am his.

Contents

✎ Prologue

Into every life some rain must fall. That rainy season occurs from the time we're in our mid-thirties to when we have more than a mid-thirty-inch waistline. It's midlife. The period that runs from the point of realization that attractive younger men now call us "ma'am," to the time when we realize that we're being nice to people just to be sure that there's a crowd at our funerals.

Midlife—it's a four-letter word ... if you're a really bad speller. But it's also extremely funny if you look at it right—or if you ignore it. Or if you sleep through as much of it as possible.

This journal chronicles my experiences from a year of midlife. Bad days, good days, bad days—yes, I meant to say that twice. This was the year I changed waist sizes twelve times, got "spayed," quit my day job, realized my cats are smarter than I am, and learned a couple of really special lessons along the way. Perhaps you have experienced similar moments. If so, we can suffer together. Or, if you haven't, I made the whole thing up.

✎ *Calooh! Callay!*

It's a brand new year. Yes, I'm a forty-something midlifer from Louisiana who lives with a multitude of stray animals, twenty-four pet dust bunnies, a rubber chicken named Elvis, and a husband named David and his pet Harley, but the year is all mine. I have a blank slate to start with and I haven't wasted a single minute.

To borrow a couple of lines from Lewis Carroll, "Oh frabjous day! Calooh! Callay!" Never knew what the heck that meant, but it seems to fit today.

I'm glad I didn't drink too much last night. I've always had an aversion to New Year's Eve parties. The idea of kissing in public at midnight, being threatened by wayward fireworks, and having a hangover on the first day of a new year never really appealed to me. But then, neither did the show *Seinfeld*, so once again, I'm obviously in the minority.

My New Year's resolutions? Maybe I'll consider my own actions and not worry about others. I will resolve to exercise and move toward my goals. Maybe I'll even try to lose this inner tube around my waist that makes me look like I'm smuggling a life preserver at all times. I'll think about all that tomorrow.

Maybe I'll write in my journal every day. This will give me a realistic view of all the accomplishments of my new year of midlife.

Yes, I have officially hit midlife, and that is a good thing, because the world is my oyster. And today I'll make cocktail sauce to go with it—heavy on the horseradish.

No work today. Today is a day for dreaming. A day for realizing that anything is possible. Calooh! Callay!

✎ New Year's Reminders

By this point in my life, I have realized that New Year's resolutions are just part of a plot by diet programs to boost sagging sales every January. But somehow that knowledge doesn't stop me from wanting to change something in my life every time I buy a new calendar.

This year, I decided to overcome that desire by creating "reminders" for myself, instead of "resolutions." As with most things in my life, these reminders range from the ridiculous to the sublime. Here is my list:

This year ...

✓ When opportunity knocks, I won't pretend I'm in the shower and refuse to answer the door.

✓ I won't wait for all the lights to turn green before setting out on new adventures.

✓ I will take a vacation before the doctor prescribes one in the form of a hospital stay.

✓ I will clean the cabinet under my sink and see if I find Mr. Hoffa.

✓ When I'm in traffic jams, instead of feeling stressed, I will pretend I'm in a parade and will wave at everyone.

✓ I will actually listen to the response I'm given after I ask people, "How are you?"

✓ When I'm in boring meetings, I will not page myself in order to escape.

✓ I will not ask, "Do I look fat in this?" If I have to ask, I already know the answer.

✓ I will not dial and drive.

✓ I will give up on those twenty-seven socks without partners.

✓ I will wash my car before kids start writing rude messages in its thick layers of dirt.

✓ I will only laugh when I mean it.

✓ I will eat dessert first if I want to.

✓ I will take steps toward my goals, even if others find my goals to be strange (Why shouldn't I want to make less money, wear more black, make my fifteen-year-old car last one more year, and make a career out of making people smile?).

✓ I will overtip.

✓ I will not consider Oreos as one of the major food groups.

✓ I will throw spitballs over the walls of my cubicle.

✓ I will not consider four-letter words to be an appropriate response to rude drivers.

✓ I will go to children's movies without children.

✓ I will stop thinking of that "fur" on my ceiling fans as an artistic statement.

✓ I will offer a silent blessing every time I pass a policeman, fireman, or veteran. And this year, it will not take a tragedy to remind me to fly my flag.

✎ Midlife Crisis 101

I thought I was already well entrenched in my midlife crisis. But something happened today that made me realize that everything that happened up to this point was just a dress rehearsal for the real thing.

I went to visit my old college campus, Louisiana State University. I spent ten of the best years of my life there earning my bachelor's degree. Don't ask.

I walked up the steps to the door of the student union building. And here, I must say, I looked good. True, I was breathing a little heavily—there were a lot of steps. But I did look good.

I had washed away the gray less than three days ago. This morning I had put on my favorite jeans, and this time they even zipped all the way up without that pooch at the top where the zipper refuses to lie flat because of the extra inches pushing from the inside. I even had on a sweatshirt with an appropriately bawdy slogan on it. Yes, I was *en vogue* today.

I reached the glass doors of the union and, from nowhere, a young fellow appeared behind me.

He flashed sky-blue eyes and grinned at me, a charming dimple appearing in his right cheek. His beard was barely stubble, but I figured at his age it was probably two months' growth. And that smile he gave said he had noticed me.

I knew at this wonderful moment that I still had "it." I could feel my face glowing. Images of *The Graduate* danced in my head. And then he said those words that I will never forget.

"Let me get that door for you, ma'am."

Ma'am. The name people use for my mother. The name I use when visiting octogenarians in the nursing home. The name that is most definitely not used on hot babes on college campuses.

I deflated my chest, released the breath I was holding to keep in my waistline, and limped forward to look for a handicapped restroom.

Thus, today my real midlife crisis began. Everything before was just a prep course.

✎ So Sue Me

Okay, so I forgot to write in my journal for a few days. What did you expect? I'm old. Forty plus. Senility could be setting in, for all I know.

How do we know when we become senile? Do we just stop asking ourselves, "Am I senile yet?" When we stop asking, does that mean we've hit senility? If that's the case, how will we remember that we've forgotten to ask the question?

While I'm asking questions, I might as well ask a few more. Why can't I decide what I want to be when I grow up? Why do I crave chocolate at least four times a week? And why isn't "that time of month" as much fun as they make it look like in maxi pad commercials? And since my tangent has already become totally unacceptable, I must admit something—I think some of this "sex stuff" must have been a big joke, courtesy of the Higher Power.

I can picture it now. Higher Power and a few friends were sitting on a cloud, bored with a perfect peaceful existence. Because of a lack of anything good on the spiritual cable channels, he decided to make up a new game. He called it "Procreation."

Higher Power: "I'll create woman, but I'll make her less sexually oriented than man. That'll be fun to watch—a constant game of begging and denial."

He enjoyed this game so much, that he decided he would go further still. "I'll make woman have attributes that the other sex likes to look at. But then, once he gets used to looking at them, I'll really confuse him. I'll shift those attributes a foot lower."

Giggling, he continued. "And then, when it's time for her to reproduce, I have a great idea for how the baby should be born."

Then the Big Kahuna* sat back and thought about his plan and started laughing so hysterically that Mrs. Kahuna had to spike his ambrosia with a little valium to calm him down. She couldn't have him getting overexcited at his age.

*Forgive me for the term Big Kahuna. I don't want to leave any religion or philosophy out and I realized that "Higher Power" just makes me think of Bill Gates. Thus, my reference to the higher being became the Big Kahuna. Politically correct or chicken, you make the call.

✎ Shiny Red Goals

Today I reviewed my list of life goals again, and once again I was embarrassed.

I remember some years ago when my husband and I first compared our revised life goals. Our earlier goals of being president and working in one of those little yellow film developing kiosks that used to be in parking lots everywhere no longer seemed realistic (I'll leave you to guess which one of us had which goal).

The first step was to sit and list the pros and cons of our old goals. Then we would research, reconsider, and do some soul-searching and other such deep considerations.

David decided to take a computer assessment test to determine what his likes and dislikes were. He researched different careers, schools, and business outlooks.

I read a couple of romance novels.

After our research, we had created our revised life goals. David had created a ten-year plan to first go back to school and get a degree in architecture, then to intern, and finally to sit for the test for his architectural license. I, on the other hand, decided to buy a shiny red car.

Ten years passed.

David is now working at a wonderful architecture firm. He's designing all sorts of structures and learning all aspects of the business. We even took a picture of him with his first project—a fire escape.

I put a new radio in the not-so-very shiny red car.

At that point we realized that we needed to update our goals again.

David decided that there were places he wanted to see in the world. So he researched possible vacation sites, studied the customs and travel regulations, and did other things an experienced traveler might do.

I read a couple more romance novels.

And then we came up with our decisions.

David recently traveled to South Africa to discover the animals in their natural habitats, to meet the Zulu people, and to find himself.

I, embarrassed into feeling that I had to do something, too, wrote a romance novel.

This midlife thing really takes a lot of energy.

✎ Random Acts of Kindness

Practice random acts of kindness and senseless beauty.

I read these words in a magazine and they really affected me. It seems that someone picked up this phrase and it started spreading through graffiti, bumper stickers, and actions. People started using it as an excuse to do terrible things like pay for the cars behind them at toll booths, leave food anonymously for less fortunate neighbors, shovel snow, and pick up trash on elderly people's property. This seemed like a pretty special idea, so yesterday, when the opportunity arose, I grabbed it.

A destitute-looking gentleman was sitting at a bus stop. His shoes were barely holding together, his jacket was threadbare, and he was discussing world economics with a geranium he was holding in soiled hands. Pausing only for a moment, I made the decision to approach him to practice my random act.

"Excuse me, sir." He looked up without expression. The geranium, on the other hand, looked impatient.

"Sir, I can't help but notice that times seem to be a little tough for you. Would you please accept this small gift? Maybe it will help a little."

He ignored the five-dollar bill I was holding out to him. "When does the bus come?"

Obviously, there were more important things on his mind. "I don't know, sir. Here, please take this." I tried again.

He stared at it confused. "That's not the bus."

Well, I was glad we had established that fact. "No, sir, it's not a bus. But it could pay for your bus ride."

"What bus ride?"

"The bus you're waiting for," I answered.

"What time does it get here?"

Hadn't he and the geranium and I already discussed this subject? "I don't know. Please take the money."

I didn't mean to be impatient with my random act, but the temperature was in the thirties, my random feelings of kindness were weakening with each moment, and I was getting nervous that the geranium might have a split personality. At that moment, a police car drove up. The officer walked over to join us at the bus stop.

"Is this man harassing you?" The officer immediately came to my aid.

"No, Officer. Actually, I guess I'm harassing him."

The policeman looked perplexed. He studied me with my frozen blue lips, the man with his vacant stare, and the suspicious geranium.

"He's selling flowers?"

"No," I answered. "I think they're related."

Now the officer looked totally confused. I explained that the gentleman needed information about the bus schedule. I didn't mention the money. I had already given up on that cause. Besides, I had noticed that the hand not holding the geranium was clutching a big roll of bills. For a moment, I thought about borrowing a couple of bucks from him.

When I finally left, the kindly officer was calling for a bus schedule for the gentleman. The man and his geranium seemed happier for the company. Although it was not in accordance with my original plan, I felt that my random act had turned out all right. I guess that's what makes it random. And I guess that's what makes me want to do it again.

✎ Discussing Personal Matters at Impersonal Times

It's amazing—people can accept the fact that you're short, you're tall, you're ugly, or you are a Democrat. But tell them that you're childless and they feel compelled to help you correct the problem, even at dinner parties like the one I attended last night.

The woman sitting next to me and I had run out of things to say, so she retreated to the typical conversation that women who have nothing in common run to.

"How long have you been married?"

"Eighteen years."

"How many little ones do you have?"

"Thirteen."

"Oh my! What are their names?"

"Fido, Harlem, Spot, Miss Kitty, Peaches, Ginger, Elvis, Shakespeare, Puck, MamaCat, Zsa Zsa, Narlee, and Tuxedo."

"Those are unusual names for children."

"They're animals."

"Well, when they're younger, they all are."

"No, they're really animals. Those are my pets."

"Oh," she said, looking distinctly relieved. "I was talking about children."

"Don't have any."

"Oh." She looked concerned again and whispered, "Is there a … *problem*?"

"No, there's no *problem*." Why did we have to whisper that word?

"Well, are you waiting to have children?"

"Nope. Don't want any."

I could have said that I enjoy the prospect of nuclear war and not gotten any more of a shocked response.

"You don't want children?"

"No."

"Why?"

Why? *Why?* Do I have to answer why I don't want Persian rugs? No. Do I have to answer why I don't like asbestos? No. But something as distinctly personal as deciding not to bear children and people feel like they can ask you to explain yourself within three minutes of meeting you.

"I'm allergic," I answered simply. I thought that would put an end to the conversation. I was wrong.

"What's wrong with children?"

"They whine, they drool, and they ask for expensive toys."

"What's wrong with that?" she asked defensively.

"Nothing. I just don't need it. I already have my husband to do those things. Besides, I'm afraid I'll be accused of child abuse."

She looked shocked. "How could you even say such a thing?"

"I'm afraid it's true. I expect children to act like adults. I would insist that they listen to old Partridge Family records with me and sit still through my stand-up comedy routines. I would probably even make them read the romance novels that I write."

"My God, you're vicious."

"I know."

"Never have children."

"If you insist."

✎ Paying the Piper and Promising Never to Buy Another Pipe

It happens every two weeks and today was the day. I sat down with the checkbook, all my bills, my calculator, and the futile hope that the right one would have a larger balance. David ran to hide. He knew that bill-paying time is usually when my manic-depressive side emerges.

I like to do what I call "creative financing." I go through the bills and see which ones are most recently overdue. I see which cards still have any credit left on them. Then I attempt to pay the most urgent bills with said credit cards, inevitably leading to a hopeless game of mix and match. Credit—the great American disaster movie.

You would think things would be great since I have a high-paying job at a large company, but somehow I always have even higher-owing bills.

And no matter how much I make, I spend it. I've tried to be responsible and save money, but then something happens and I have to waste those savings on something silly like an operation, a plumbing repair, or a really big stereo system.

The last time I had money saved was right before the flood of 1987. I remember waking up to a foot of water in my house, only to open the bedroom door to find my perturbed cat floating in her litter box and my computer screen peeking out from under the waves where it was sitting on the floor. I woke my husband up with, "Dear, how much do you have left in that elementary school savings account that you never closed out?" It was after that flood that I decided that saving money is just a waste. You only end up spending your money on useful things instead of fun stuff.

So I generally put aside the bills that can wait. I keep them in a little box I have until it's time to pay them. Or I keep them in that little box until I forget them and get that nasty letter from the company.

At some point during the process this morning, my husband ventured forth and popped his head into the room. "How's it going?"

He's always careful to keep from being trapped in the room with me when I'm doing bills. He knows I'm apt to shout obscenities from time to time. He knows I'll bug him about why he isn't in a high-paying job like used car sales. But today was better. We actually both have jobs this week.

I was able to smile weakly. "We may not have to cook the dog this week."

He was relieved.

"However, barbecuing the parrot is not yet out of the question."

He was slightly less relieved. "Is it bad?"

"Not as bad as it could be. We've just got to stop spending money. Do you think we could do without eating for a few weeks? It would really help."

He thought it over.

Whenever times were at their toughest, we usually ended up selling something to pay bills. This was a sort of self-inflicted punishment for overspending. However, times were tough a lot. Especially during that "I'm going to be a stand-up comic for a living" era. They knew us by name at the local classified paper. And we were down to a very scant few items of any worth remaining in our house.

I ventured to bring up this solution. "Is there something that we could sell?"

He immediately looked at my pinball machine.

"No." I was vehement. "That is my pride and joy."

"You haven't played on it in three years."

"Sure I have."

"Then why haven't you noticed that the cat ate the ball out of it three years ago?"

"Well, that explains why I haven't gotten many points in my last games."

He was skeptical. "So selling that is out?"

I nodded. "What about your drums?"

He was taken aback. "How can you even suggest that? Those drums were my livelihood for years. They've been my prized possession since high school. They don't even make that brand anymore."

"You haven't played them in five years."

"Yes, but I could if I wanted to."

"They're so big, they won't fit in any of our rooms."

"I could play in a band again. Picture it—the remaining Beatles do a reunion tour and throw Ringo out so I can be their drummer. If I didn't have any drums, where would I be then?"

I relented. How can you argue with logic that includes the Beatles? I put aside the bills. They'll be there tomorrow. I plugged in the pinball machine and started searching for a marble to replace the lost ball. My husband began adjusting his snare drum.

Sure, we're poor, but take away our toys and we're poor and bored. I'd rather be just plain poor.

Wednesday, February 14

✎ Valentine's Dance

This is that time of year when we're bombarded with beautiful people on television sharing thousand-dollar diamond illustrations of their love. On one show he's taking her on a cruise. On a commercial, he's spent a month's salary on a pair of earrings. On a nighttime drama, she shows her affection by granting him the divorce he wants.

And here we are, the real people of the world celebrating Valentine's Day, just thrilled if the pizza arrives on time.

The good thing about midlife is when you realize that it's what's inside that matters.

No, not in the way your mother told you about when you went through that ugly prepubescent stage where zits stood out farther than your nose. In the real way. Like when you look at your chubby husband with the receding hairline and it makes you want to peer down to check if you can see your feet today. And you realize that it hasn't been a bad hair day—it's been a bad hair month. When it hits you that everyone who is considered beautiful on television is at least one decade younger than you.

But then he looks at you and you see something in your partner's eyes.

"What are you looking at?" I was automatically on the defensive, checking for an offending element hanging from my nose.

"My wife."

What does he mean by that? Is this a joke? I said to myself, while trying to look into his eyes and into his thoughts. He knows me well enough to realize what I was thinking.

"No punch line here."

"Why would you look at me?"

"I like what I see."

"Well, I did actually dust."

"Not the shelf behind you. You."

"I'm so fat."

"If you want to change something about you, change it for you, not for me, because I really like what I see."

I was still waiting for the joke. "How could you like me? There are beautiful young women all over the place. Most of the world is younger than me now."

"Youth," he shook his head. "Been there, done that, got the free radio station T-shirt."

"Wouldn't you like me to be younger? Thinner? Less hormonal?"

"You were. It was fun then. But I like the way you are now."

"But..."

"There aren't any buts here. Wouldn't you like me to be younger, thinner, and less focused on buying a Harley?"

I looked at him. There was a reflection in his eyes that I really like. Sure, he wasn't wearing his glasses and that's probably why he thought I looked okay, but there was something more there.

Then he did something I never expected. He punched the button on his CD player and the silly man found the song that I picked to be played at our wedding. A little known tune with the line, "Where would I be without your love?" He held his hand out and took mine and pulled me close. And we danced in circles in the small area of the room behind his computer desk.

You know what? I don't want to be young. I don't want to be thin. I don't care what hormones kick in tomorrow. This is exactly where I want to be.

For a moment, we were both skinny, long-haired kids in the seventies, thinking about the future together, and laughing about the way we were stepping on each other's toes.

Valentine's Day. Television networks haven't got a clue.

Monday, February 19

✎ Who's Holding the Camera?

We were watching a documentary earlier tonight about a lonely expedition that a single man attempted to make up the side of an unbelievably brutal mountain. The isolation. The danger. The fear. But we were watching it on television, so I wondered, who's holding the camera?

I addressed this concern to my husband. "If he's supposed to be alone, who's taking the pictures?"

"This might just be a reenactment."

"Then why don't they have a disclaimer across the bottom of the screen that says so? They used to have to do that on the news when they did those *CrimeStoppers* things where they reenacted crimes."

He shrugged. Yeah, like that was going to discourage me from talking.

"And do you wonder if those people who reenact crimes on shows like *America's Most Wanted* ever get attacked by citizens on the streets who want the reward money? Or maybe they have the police called on them all the time."

"We all have job hazards." My husband was trying hard to concentrate on his PBS special.

"What if a former crime reenactment actor got a job in a television commercial? That could be detrimental to the product's image."

"Do you stay up at night thinking of these things?" My husband was obviously astonished at the depth of my logic.

"No, they just come to me on the spur of the moment."

He was just staring at me now, the television show completely forgotten.

Enjoying this moment of his undivided attention, I continued, "I always wonder why cameramen don't help their subjects more often. When poor salmon are being filmed trying to swim upstream, why don't we see a cameraman's hand sneak into the side of the picture and give them a little extra push? And what crazed photographer stayed behind to get those close-up pictures of tornadoes?"

Seeing that David was still listening to me, I continued. "And how come people don't notice those hidden cameras in those on-the-spot interviews? I mean, she's sitting there with some guy asking her about a product and a few feet behind him is a two-way mirror where she can hear a belching cameraman cursing, 'You forgot the fries?' Don't you think this interview subject could put two and two together and get Tuesday?"

"Completely amazing." This was murmured as, having given up on the mountain documentary, he had turned the channel to try to watch close-up pictures of some reddish-colored planet.

"A planet, huh?"

"Yes."

"Who's taking the picture?"

"Unmanned probe."

"Maybe that's what they used on the mountain."

"I doubt it," he answered, but upon seeing my confusion, he tried to help. "Maybe it's Bigfoot."

That satisfied me. When all else fails in our home, Bigfoot is always a good explanation.

Television is much too confusing. Real life is simpler. Like in our annual family photograph, it's easy to tell who's taking the picture. It's the person whose head is glued onto the photo.

Thursday, February 22

✎ A Seminar in Time Management

Time management is an interesting concept. We have time and we have things to do, and we actually think we can put the two together in some sort of useful and productive manner. And then we are assaulted by the real world.

As director of training at my company, part of my job is teaching adults things they don't want to learn, so it's easy to see how important it is for me to set a good example by being organized. With my handy little day planner book open today, I actually felt organized and ready to go. My appointments were all listed in the monthly calendar. I had noted them in my weekly schedule and had even placed them on my daily agenda. I was sitting in my office at the precise moment an appointment was to occur when the unthinkable happened. An unscheduled phone call came in.

It was my next-door neighbor. "Your house is being robbed."

"What?" Sure, I heard what she said, but you're always supposed to say "what" when you hear startling news. This social custom was probably developed by a nation of people who had one too many practical jokes played on them.

"Your house is being robbed," she repeated.

"How do you know?"

"Well, did you order a U-Haul with four men in turbans to break in your back door and remove your television today?"

"Hold on." I grabbed my day planner. "No, it's not on my schedule."

"Then my guess would be that they're robbing you."

"They can't do that," I informed her. "It's not on my schedule for today. I might have time for them to rob me later this week, but I've got appointments all day today."

"What are you going to do?" As she was speaking, I heard the shattering of glass in the background. The neighborhood watch group must have been on vacation. I jotted down a reminder in my planner to speak to the director.

"That was my ceramic vase from the living room, wasn't it?"

"Is it a tall, white thing with black and blue flowers?"

"Yes."

"Good ear."

"I'm not sure what to do. I don't really have time to call the police. I have a list of phone calls already made up for today, and the police station is not on it."

"Maybe you should revise your list."

"If I do that, the whole week will be messed up."

"Oh look, there goes that darling little lamp I gave you for Christmas."

That made me angry. I showed up at the house in less than ten minutes. Four large, swarthy men were struggling with my entertainment center. They froze as I marched up to the truck. "What the heck do you think you're doing?"

Through a thick accent, the smallest of the men, probably only six feet five inches tall, spoke up first. "We are moving furniture."

"Try again, Hassan. I live here. Furniture moving is not on my schedule for today," I said, pointing at my day planner for emphasis.

He seemed to consider this, then opted for the truth. "We are stealing your things."

"Now that's more like it. The truth will make this planning process much easier. Okay, on my schedule for today, I only have thirty spare minutes. I hardly believe that thirty minutes is enough time for you to steal everything of value from my home and then for me to call the police, file a report, and have you tracked down and thrown in jail. Don't you think this is a reasonable assumption?"

Hassan nodded nervously. He obviously had not thought through this schedule very well.

"I have an answer," I informed him. He looked relieved. "You put everything back where you found it. Prop the door back in place. Then call me at my office at 2:17 this afternoon. I'll look on my schedule for the week and see when I have time to be robbed. And I'll try to pencil you in. Okay?"

When I left they had everything back in the house and were trying to glue the vase back together. I was proud because I had taught another person the value of time management.

✎ I Don't Own the Road, But I Do Rent a Lane From Time to Time

This afternoon my husband and I decided to finally run some of the errands we'd been putting off. Upon leaving the house, I sat down in my car, for which one hundred fifty thousand miles is just a distant memory. The car that flies from zero to sixty in just under a weekend. And from somewhere, I heard the distant chant of, "Let the games begin."

"C'mon, let's move it. Nothing to see here. What are you waiting for, Christmas?" I was extremely vocal. My husband just smiled. You see, we hadn't left the driveway yet.

Now, I am basically a sane person. In fact, I am normally rather timid. But put me inside those thousands of pounds of metal and I become a snarling, vicious vigilante of the roads. It is my duty to make the roads safe for all mankind by warning drivers if they are not good enough to be operating a vehicle. And don't even get me started on my "Don't Dial and Drive" campaign.

Here's how our nice little drive went today.

My husband noticed that I was watching the rearview mirror more than the road in front of me.

"Not again," he moaned. He knew what this meant. It meant that behind me "Mr. Inconsiderate Driver" was insisting on driving much too close to my antique vehicle. And my husband knew that it was now my duty to tell this driver that he was too close.

I began with the classic "flailing arm" move. This is a wave that either tells the driver that there is a wasp in my car or that he should move back.

The driver apparently did not understand.

Next, I attempted the "Look at my brake lights" move by tapping my brakes. The driver, who appeared to be eating a twelve-course breakfast, did not notice.

Finally, I moved on to the most drastic of my warning signals. Yes, I turned backward to face the driver in the car behind me and mouthed the words, "Get back."

The driver, noting that I was no longer looking at the road in front of me, was alarmed into backing off from my car. And I was satisfied. My husband, on the other hand, had passed out.

It was probably for the best. Errands are usually easier to get done when he's not around anyway.

✎ Television Trivia or Trivial Television?

Tonight I spent two hours trying to find something to watch on television. I feel like I had more of a choice back when we had only three networks and a test pattern. Honestly, sometimes when I'm watching a show like *Who Wants to Be an Apprentice Millionaire Nanny Survivor*, I really miss that test pattern.

I spent the formative years of my life in front of a black-and-white television with rabbit ear antennae. Inevitably, this led to deep thoughts and unanswerable questions.

I remember *Gilligan's Island* and I wonder why the Howells took their entire wardrobe along for a three-hour cruise. And why didn't the group put Gilligan's head on a stake after he had ruined the hundredth rescue attempt? And really, how could they complete scientific experiments and build radio receivers and earthquake-measuring instruments, but never manage to create a simple raft that could carry them into the shipping lanes?

And on *Star Trek*, why did the Starship Enterprise's five-year mission only last two and a half seasons? I remember how on every show, Scotty would say, "But Cap'n, the ship's engines can't take much more." Why didn't anybody consider that Scotty might just have been a really bad engineer?

Furthermore, what kind of mother would call her son The Beaver?

Did they think we wouldn't notice on *Bewitched* when Dick York turned into Dick Sergeant? And why did Oliver

Wendell Douglas keep buying stuff from Mr. Haney on *Green Acres*?

Then there was the classic, *Wild Kingdom*. My parents admired Marlin Perkins, but I just wondered why Jim had to do all the dirty work. Marlin would say, "Now Jim will tackle this alligator. This is one of my trickier jobs."

What's tricky, Marlin? You're in the helicopter with a bullhorn suggesting that Jim show the camera the side of his head without the blood.

I loved Ed Sullivan. However, his hunched back and insistence on pronouncing the word "show" as "shoe" bothered me slightly.

Looking back, I can see that television was an indicator to my future. I guess I should have known that humor would play a huge role in my life when I realized that the man on television I had a crush on was not Clark Gable, Errol Flynn, or Humphrey Bogart. It was Red Skelton.

✎ Tae Kwon Don't

This evening David practiced his Tae Kwon Do in our living room. It was fascinating to watch him punch, kick at a spot somewhere above his head, and yell "keyhop" (not to be confused with "carhop"). I found his efforts especially enjoyable because I was able to watch him from my comfy couch with a glass of wine and an array of extremely fattening food items all within my reach.

"You're wearing me out," I noted as I strained to pick up a heavy chip loaded with dip.

"Sorry." He's always so agreeable.

"No problem." I watched as he kicked above his head again. "That's great."

"Really?" He looked pleased.

"Yes. Now I don't have to go get a flyswatter when there's a spider high up on the wall."

"Not exactly what the kick is designed for, but I'm flexible," he said, shrugging.

"What exactly is all this designed for?" I asked this because not only was I intrigued, I was in between sitcoms.

"It's for self-defense. But you should avoid using it unless absolutely necessary."

"So you're learning something that, if you're successful, you should never have to use."

"Essentially, yes."

"That makes a lot of sense to me," I said, nodding.

"You're being facetious, aren't you?"

"Me?" I was flabbergasted. "When have I ever been facetious?"

"When have you been breathing?" He smiled.

"Harrumph." Well, I said something along that line. I don't remember exactly. The wine was kicking in.

"Actually, it wouldn't hurt at all for you to learn a few martial arts moves," he informed me. "It can really help you protect yourself in dangerous situations."

"I'm game. Teach me." This was definitely the wine speaking.

He helped me up from the couch. Once we'd gotten past this twenty-minute process, we were ready for training. He turned me around so that I was facing away from him and put his arm across my neck.

"Now, if I did this to you, where could you hit me that would hurt the most?"

It took only an instant for me to come up with the answer. "Your pocketbook. Alimony."

"Not exactly the spot I was thinking of."

"Oops. I guess that was a marital arts thing, not martial arts."

"Well, your humor could knock them out, but let's try something else." He then demonstrated a series of places where I could hit an attacker, including the instep, the arm, the neck, and various other spots he called "pressure points."

"These are a lot like the Vulcan Death Grip that Spock did on *Star Trek*," I noted.

"Yes, whatever." He agreed, but I know it was just to keep me practicing. "Pressure points can temporarily disable a person so you can get away."

"Yeah. I guess the alimony thing wouldn't work on an attacker unless I married him first."

"Different kind of punishment," he muttered.

In his defense, I think he was trying to goad me into attacking. It worked. I pulled out my worst weapon. "Honey, I think I feel a depressed mood coming on."

It was then that we figured it out—the best weapon ever. This morning I made a new button to wear that simply says, "I'm out of my Prozac." I feel so safe ... and no one will ever make me wait in line at the store anymore.

✎ Don't Stop Me if I've Told You This Story Before

I found myself looking for wrinkles today. For the first time, I really found them. They're not laugh lines anymore. They're out and out wrinkles. But I realized that if I'm getting old, I want to do a few things to make it worth my while.

I want to get to that point where it doesn't bother me that I am telling the same story to the same person for the twelfth time.

The point where the discomfort of Mugger Underwear (i.e., underwear that creeps up on you from behind) outweighs the modesty that used to prevent me from yanking it down to its proper station in full view of a store security camera.

My mom and I are just about at that point. We're in that hazy, gray area somewhere between the underwear twist and "Grandma's talking to the ficus bush again."

Senility. I figure that if you start acting crazy early enough in life, no one will know when you actually hit it. Mom and I have decided to write a book about it called *Journal of a Senility Crisis.* To reinforce our theme, we agreed that we would repeat the prologue every third chapter.

I used to think that telling the same story over and over was a sign of senility, but now I know better. It is simply a testament to the fact that a good story is always a good story. Why bother coming up with new good stories when there's a perfectly good one using up space in the gray matter of our brain?

Or at least, that's what Mom taught me.

Mom loves to tell the story of my birthday ... the original one. She was sharing a hospital room with a lovely blonde woman who was also "in a family way." Hours later (many, many hours, about which she has recounted to me numerous times, including every single labor pain, burp, and groan), they both had their babies in hand.

Oddly enough, the little blonde woman had a dark-haired, dark-eyed child, while my dark-haired mother was holding a blonde-haired, blue-eyed infant. Her concern led her to call the nurse.

"Are you sure you didn't switch the babies?"

"Honey," the nurse rolled her eyes, "your husband has already had us checking footprints and everything else. This one's yours."

It was months before my hair and eyes finally turned dark like the rest of the family's. Up until then, both Mom and Dad were still trying to return me to the hospital. Of course, once my nose grew the mandatory extra two feet, thanks to my Lebanese heritage, they had to reluctantly admit that I was their offspring.

Why can I tell this story as if I were there? Simple. I have now heard my mother tell this story 16,347 times. Amazingly, with this story, the facts have stayed rather constant. Her other stories have not been so lucky. For instance, the other day she told me about how things were when she was young.

"I remember the tough times of World War I," Mom began.

"You weren't born then," I reminded her.

"That makes it a little harder to remember, but not impossible," she assured me.

I stood corrected. She continued.

"It was almost as bad as the Depression."

"You were four years old then." I shouldn't have even wasted my breath. She was on a roll. She glared and kept going.

"I was a mature four-year-old. I was working at the fax center of a Kinko's."

Yes, the whole notion was ridiculous, but I didn't bother to correct her. Even though I knew good and well that I was the one who worked at Kinko's fax center when I was four.

✎ Getting Older

Yes, I'm definitely getting older.

David walked into the living room this evening as I was watching one of those teen dramas that come on every night and is either named for zip codes or other location tips.

"David, I'm officially old."

"And you figured this out because..."

"I'm watching a teen show."

"That would seem to indicate that you're young at heart."

"No. I'm lusting after the father on the show."

"Ewww."

That was his best response?

"There's a supposedly hunky young son on this show and all I can think is that he doesn't even have facial hair yet."

"No chest hair either." He smiled and pulled at the buttons on his shirt to show the forest growing there.

"Yeah, yeah. You're a grizzly."

"You could be a little more enthusiastic."

"Good grizzly." He apparently didn't understand that this conversation was about me.

"What do you want me to say?"

"I don't know. I'm sure there's something very reassuring you could mention here."

"Okay. Let me think." He screwed up his face. "How about you like the father because your taste is maturing?"

"No. We've used the maturing excuse for the fact that I wear one-piece bathing suits with skirts."

"Okay. How about this? You like the father because all the other people on the show are way too young?"

"Nope. We used that excuse when I realized all the NFL players were younger than me."

"Well," he looked closely at the television screen, "the father does look okay. And that son is too skinny. Maybe that's why you like the father."

"No good."

"We used that one?"

"People are too skinny nowadays," I quoted. "We used that rationalization when I realized that all the NFL players weighed less than me."

"Oh yeah. The start of the cabbage soup diet."

"And those fainting episodes that went with it."

"So how do I help—" He stopped in mid-sentence.

"What? What is it?"

He stopped and cocked his head to one side. "You know, the mom on this show has a nice butt."

Thank goodness. I guess his taste is maturing, too. But I won't let him get away with noticing rear ends. "Well, that's just gross."

Tuesday, March 6

✎ Car Shopping

Being the sort of driver that I am, I have to be sensible in my choice of cars. I always get four doors so that the dog and cats will have their own entrances. I prefer small cars, so when I have wrecks I don't block two lanes. I like having an old car, so that my slight miscalculations on the distance to telephone poles don't upset me too much.

But recently I have begun to think about the need for a new car. A person going through a midlife crisis should not be allowed to look at cars. At the car lot today my eyes alighted on a little black convertible. My husband cringed.

"It's standard," he noted.

"I'll learn to drive it."

"The last time I tried to teach you to drive standard you forgot to look at the road."

"You're just upset because I ran over your parents' poodle. He did fine with that pin in his hip."

"No. It was actually your running over my mom's foot while she was petting the poodle that upset me."

"She did fine with that pin in her foot." I changed the subject. "I'd rather have a silver car anyway. Let's see if they have it in silver."

The salesman seemed stunned. "Is color really that important?" he asked.

I haven't laughed that hard since that chair broke Geraldo's nose.

"Is color important?" I snorted, which is not a pretty thing to do when you have a nose the size of mine. "Is color important? What else do you look at when you choose a car? Certainly you don't expect us to really look at all that nonsense on horsepower and engine and reliability. It's the color that matters."

I decided I didn't want to buy a car there, because this man had upset me with his flippant remark. Besides they did not have the cute little car in silver.

But still I walked around the lot, looking for something practical, but really cheap. Something that had personality. Something that wasn't so pretty that I would get attached to it and be upset when I took down my next mailbox in it. Something like ...

I saw it, and before I knew it, I had driven away in it. Sure, it was my own car. But I got a great deal on it.

✎ A Lady Named Bertha

I was feeling particularly yuppie and pretty darn self-important last week. I was flying to San Francisco for business meetings, during which I would teach other yuppie, self-important businesspeople professional and personal skills in the workplace. While on the plane I worked on my laptop computer and drank a bottle of mineral water. I had the latest John Grisham novel with me. Then I remembered my last trip to San Francisco and how I met a lady named Bertha and suddenly everything jumped back into perspective.

Bertha is thirty-five-feet long and weighs about twelve hundred pounds for each foot of length. But she doesn't look chubby. In fact, she carries her weight quite well.

Bertha is a gray whale. And she is the lady who made me realize how unimportant I truly am. However, since she didn't immediately claim me as a relative, she also made me see that I'm not as overweight as I thought I was.

But I'm getting ahead of myself.

Last year I decided to go on a whale watch expedition in San Francisco. Thousands of gray whales migrate each year from Alaska to Baja, California (and I thought my vacations were tough). Groups of crazed people like me jump on little boats and travel out into the ocean each day to try to spot these creatures.

The tour guides suggested seasick medication. But, of course, I am a toughie and don't need that sort of thing. About thirty minutes into the ride in the choppy Pacific Ocean, I was turning interesting shades of chartreuse. My whale-watching friends noted this.

"Are you always that color?" The little old lady from Mississippi wearing the fiberglass foot cast asked.

The old man from Florida shook his head. "She wasn't that color when we got on here."

"It's probably one of them danged new makeup fads," a woman in a pith helmet noted.

I just forced a smile. I wasn't sure what would happen if I opened my mouth to speak.

"Do you think she's seasick?"

"The guide said they don't call it seasickness anymore. It's acute gastric distress," the New Yorker informed us knowingly. "Oh no, wait, it's acute abdominal distress. Or is it a cute abominable in a dress?"

"Sure looks like seasickness to me." The fellow from Texas called it as he saw it.

But all talk of acute green distress was gone the instant we heard a spewing sound nearby. Fifty people, from telemarketers to executives to retirees to a green-faced tomboy, were instantly transformed from land-dwellers into rejects from a bad movie version of *Moby Dick*. In one voice we screamed, "Thar she blows!" and from that moment the magic took over.

We crushed toward the sides of the boat and watched in amazement as three gray whales treated us to a display of majesty. As they would get near the surface, a turquoise haze would appear in the water. And then they would roll upward and spew water toward the heavens. Once a tail even appeared. Or a "fluke", as we seafaring types would call it.

We each had our own approach to try to attract the whales. I whistled and called, "Here whale, here boy." I didn't understand the lack of response. The size of the whale's stomach reminded me of my dog's, and she always responds to that.

The man next to me was silent. Obviously a leftover response from having to stay quiet while fishing.

The little old lady in the cast was hanging off the side of the boat, clutching her water-soaked camera and yelling at the waves to get out of the way so she could get a good shot.

And every time these creatures rolled upward and made their presence known, we all cheered, yelled, clapped, and danced about like children. And, for a few moments, a group that had nothing more in common than an abundance of Dramamine and drenched clothing understood what it meant to be united by nature.

As I continued on into San Francisco for my meetings, I felt a little more humble and a little less self-important. I hope Bertha's out there somewhere reminding another unsuspecting tourist what it feels like to suddenly see the bigger picture.

✎ Surgery ... Beep, Beep

Well, I finally did it. I had "female" surgery. Or, as David so daintily puts it, I got spayed. Actually, it was just a cheap way to get a six-week vacation, but a girl's gotta do what a girl's gotta do!

A couple weeks ago, I finally looked into my two-year problem. Doctor Number Three decided to do an ultrasound and other medical-sounding tests. She discovered (and this should be sung to the tune of "The Twelve Days of Christmas") four fibroid tumors and a polyp on my endometrium. Nothing malignant, just a bunch of stuff growing where it shouldn't. Ironically, I can't get a darn houseplant to grow for anything.

But I must admit, my hospital stay hasn't been too bad. They gave me a little pump thingy that I just push when I feel pain and it beeps as it puts more painkiller into my IV. That beep is now my favorite sound. It's like Pavlov's dog. I have a feeling that from now on the sound of the microwave will lull me into a deep sleep.

Being in the hospital brings up interesting thoughts—or maybe it's the medication. But something makes me wonder... Why do they wake us up to give us sleeping pills? Why do nurses say "we" when they ask us things, like, "Have we been to the bathroom yet? How are we feeling? Why are we singing 'beep, beep' all the time?" I would prefer to handle all these things alone, thank you.

And I don't know why people complain about catheters. After this episode, I think I'll want to recreate this experience with adult diapers. Watching an entire baseball game without a trip to the bathroom sounds pretty good to me.

I kept dozing off as people talked to me. I've lost a meal or two because of my stomach's reaction to the beeps. And I can barely form a coherent thought.

All in all, it's the best vacation I've had in about five years. Beep. Beep.

✎ Putting Off the Decision to Procrastinate

I just looked at my to-do list. It has 337.5 items on it. I might get to the .5 today.

I put things off so much, I bought a self-improvement tape to help. It's called *Doing It Now.* Then I put off listening to it for two months.

My procrastination comes naturally. My mother put off having me until she already had five other children.

Last week I finally listened to the tape I bought. It instructed me to break things down into smaller tasks and then take them step-by-step. This part was easy. However, I may have broken things down a little too much. The first thing on my list was waking up. Then there was breathing. Then there was sitting up. I'd been doing one small task on my list every day for the entire week and I'd only worked my way up to sitting on the edge of the bed.

These lists are dangerous. The average human being can easily become addicted to lists, and the surgeon general never even warned us that this would happen. We list-addicts find ourselves making lists to remind us to look at our lists.

I once worked with a girl who made the mistake of using the same list for home and work. Then she made the bigger mistake of leaving it in full view at work. We saw that she woke up at 6:30. She got out of bed at 6:31. She went to the bathroom at 6:32. She got into the shower at 6:35. One day when she made us particularly mad, we erased her nightly visit to the bathroom off her list.

My lists have helped me a little with my procrastination problem. Had I made these lists all along, I might have been more organized. And, had I been more organized, there are things I probably would have done differently in my life.

For example, had I made a list to remind me to go to class, college wouldn't have been the best ten years of my life; it may have only been the best six or eight. Had I made lists to remind me to watch the news once in a while, I might have known that taking a blue dress with a yogurt stain on it to the dry cleaners would have had political overtones. If I had made a list to remind me not to be a nerd, I would have started using the word "groovy" in the seventies when everyone else was using it, instead of waiting until last year.

But then again, maybe everything would have turned out exactly the same way. I might still have been a professional college student using outdated language, but I would just have a whole bunch of lists shoved into my pocket protector.

There are other people who could have profited from making these lists. Lincoln could have worked his plans to go to an earlier feature of the play. Joan of Arc could have stopped putting off buying that asbestos underwear. Thomas Edison could have invented the phonograph earlier so that we could have all been listening to rap records decades sooner. On the other hand, some procrastination is a good thing.

And then, I occasionally realize that I am not alone in my procrastination. On Mother's Day last year, I found myself in a store checkout line behind fifteen people holding wilted Mother's Day flower arrangements. Number sixteen didn't count. He had a memorial wreath. Said his mother was still alive, but it was all he could find and he figured she could use it on him when she realized he had forgotten her special day again.

At one point I considered the idea of forming a Procrastinators Anonymous. But I decided that everyone would put off joining and I could only imagine how many members would be late for the meetings. So, while there are hundreds of thousands of us, we must continue to suffer alone.

At least I know that when I finally pass away, they'll be using the right word to describe me—the *late* Christee Gabour Atwood.

✎ Want Fries With That?

Shannon, a friend from work, called me today and we talked about silly things like dreams and goals and all that nonsense, and somewhere along the way, I realized that I'm backward. It's a little sad.

"My goal is to make enough money to retire by the time I'm fifty," this ambitious young lady told me. "I'm going to be married and have my two kids and live by the country club."

"Nice." I smiled into the phone. It was one of those knowing smiles that only come when those of us who are past forty are talking to those who haven't yet even visited thirty-land.

"What about you?"

Why is it that young people expect interaction on phone calls? My mother calls and she does not expect me to talk. Doesn't even encourage it. It's her nickel and she's going to tell me everything she needs to. If I wanted to talk, I'd make the call and she wouldn't get the chance to talk. But the girl was waiting.

"By the time I'm fifty, I plan to have paid off my MasterCard from college."

"But what else?"

She wanted me to think of a bigger goal than paying off a twenty-year-old MasterCard? This girl needed a reality check. But I had nothing better to do, so we continued the conversation.

"And I plan to get a job that allows me to say things like, 'Would you like fries with that?'"

"How could you want that? You're head of the department." She was shocked. I suppose I would have been, too, when I was in my twenties and thought the presidency was my next natural step in careers.

"Yup. I'm working in this job because I had debts that only a big paycheck could handle—because I thought I had to keep up with the Joneses and the Trumps. But somewhere along the way I learned something."

"And that was?" Kids are so impatient. I was trying to tell a story in the old-fashioned Jimmy Stewart method and she wanted the MTV quick sound-bites version.

"There are things that are more important. My vision of success doesn't have to be like anyone else's. I can choose my own. I don't need to be rich to be happy. Sometimes it's more fun to be poor and creative."

"But don't you want money?"

"I'm not stupid. Sure, I'd take it. But it's not a goal. It's a sideline. If I let money be my goal, I'll never stop moving and fighting. And I'll always be angry with people who seem to be getting more than their share. As it is, I'm pleasantly surprised with whatever comes my way."

"That doesn't make any sense."

"Not when you're twenty, it doesn't." I smiled one of those knowing smiles again. "Gotta go. I've got an important meeting."

"Aha! A meeting. See, you're doing something for your career, even when you say you don't care."

"Yeah, maybe you're right." I laughed and hung up the phone to prepare for my meeting. I put on my tennis shoes, grabbed my cat, and walked out into the backyard. We immediately jumped into the subject of our meeting—an unruly leaf that needed to be attacked.

Yup, you just can't explain it. You have to get there on your own.

✎ Interpreting those Pesky Tax Forms

Yes, it's that wonderful time of year. The birds are singing. The flowers are starting to bloom. I've almost recovered from my March Mardi Gras party. And it's time to help Uncle Sam afford a new $500 toilet seat—yes, it's tax time.

What an ugly experience. For poor people, we sure paid a lot of taxes. I pulled out all the forms. I sharpened my pencil. And here's how I have learned to interpret the questions on these forms:

Name: Use your real name. This is not the time to put Bubba or Hot Mama. The government frowns on this because they already have 2,213 Bubbas and 472 Hot Mamas working for them and it would get confusing if there were any more of them.

Filing Status: The IRS is not like your mother. They don't expect an explanation if you mark "Single."

Number of exemptions: The formula for this is simple. Multiply the number of people in your house by the number of cellular telephones. Then add the number of pets minus the cat that Aunt Phoebe ran over last week. Multiply it all by 1.5. Then put 2 in the blank.

Occupation: This is not the time to put the job you do for Uncle Cletus on weekends during hunting season that involves that bootlegging still in Kisatchie Forest. Put down what you do when you go to work on Monday morning.

Do you want to donate to the presidential campaign fund? This is not the time to use expletives. A simple "no" will suffice.

Donations: Please note that money you gave to your cousin Podie to get him to leave your house is not a valid deduction (unless Podie runs a home for wayward women on the side).

Reminders to self:

✓ "Gross Income" is an accounting term. It's not a description of how bad your salary is.

✓ If Line 13C is larger than 14C, simply send all the money in your pockets, checking account, savings account, the keys to your car, and your first-born to the government.

✓ Deducting the use of your cat as a business expense hardly ever floats with the IRS.

✓ If you file on the internet, avoid putting those little smiley faces people make with colons and parentheses anywhere on the form.

✓ If you fill out Form C, remember that just because you lost money this year when that brilliant new Pocket Potato Peeler didn't work, you still can't list your business as a non-profit.

✓ Filing for an extension is not the same thing as asking them to send you some hair braids.

✓ No matter how many forms you fill out, the last one will always tell you to go back and redo them all in Portuguese.

And the most important thing to remember is that it's only money. There are more important things like family, friends, and good deeds. And that's good because these are usually the only things we can afford to enjoy on April 16.

✎ Putting the Fun Back in Funerals

When I was younger, I used to want people to be happy when I died. I wanted them to have a party. I wanted no depression whatsoever.

Time went on and I began to rethink this concept. Today I decided that when I die, I want a great sadness to fall over the land. Yes, I want there to be a great weeping and wailing, gnashing of teeth, and the "renting" of garments, preferably tuxedos.

I have pictured my funeral. The mourners file slowly past my casket, saying things like, "She looks lovely," "She was so talented," and "What a loss the world has suffered." Males from my past would say, "I always had a crush on her."

But then, from nowhere, my eighth-grade teacher would appear, saying, "I expected so much more from her. But no, she ended up being a writer. Why, the IRS doesn't even recognize that as a real occupation!"

With this one negative statement, it would be like someone just said that the emperor was buck-naked. Suddenly people would have the nerve to say what they really thought.

"In all her life, she probably only stopped talking for thirteen minutes."

"She had that annoying sniffle that drove me crazy."

"She owed me eight dollars."

Then my funeral would take on the flavor of a roast.

Every negative thing from my past would come rushing out to haunt me. The eulogy would turn into bad one-liners.

Then someone would bring up the condition of my house. "Do you realize that when she died, she did not appear to have dusted in the last decade?"

And of course, since your mother teaches you to wear nice underwear in case you're in an accident, that would somehow come into play in this funeral.

"She was wearing a pair of underwear from her junior high school days when the ambulance picked her up. She fought the hospital emergency room people off, insisting she would rather die than let them see her happy face undies. We estimate that she hadn't washed her clothes since Nixon was in office."

And since this funeral in my mind has become so bizarre, it could only get worse. I notice that I'm wearing the one thing in my closet that I really hate, and that it's inside out.

At this point in my mental funeral, I'm pretty disgusted. In fact, I decide that even weeping and wailing wouldn't be enough to make my funeral satisfactory—I'm just going to have to live forever. Besides, I could never pick out an outfit I would be happy with for eternity. Even dead people deserve to be fickle.

Since I'm already on the subject of funerals, let me say that there should be a manual of things not to say at these events. The worst has got to be, "She looks so natural." This is the biggest insult to the deceased since somebody told her she didn't sweat much for a fat girl. She would only look natural if the only time you saw her in life was when she was passed out in a crate.

Or how about, "She looks so peaceful?" What, you think she'd be sitting up in there making plans to overthrow the government?

Then there are people who explain to their youngster, "Yes, Junior, she's asleep." Great. Now the kid is afraid to go to sleep for the rest of his preschool years.

Actually, I don't always say the right things at funerals either. I tend to slip up and say things like, "Nice broach.

You're not going to bury that thing, are you?" And so, I usually end up staying home. People seem to appreciate it from me.

✎ Crossing Over and Under

I found this great book at the bookstore today where deceased people talk to their loved ones through mediums. Sure, it bothers me a little that when I write the great American novel, I'll not only be competing with other contemporary authors, but also a bunch of contemporary dead people. But I'm really happy that people are starting to say out loud that our loved ones who have passed are still with us. I believe it. I enjoy talking to Grandma, Uncle Larry, and old friends more and more often now. The only problem is the flip side.

I now find it necessary to remind my late Uncle Sam not to look when I'm in the bathroom. And I feel the need to explain my actions to my dead relatives. "I'm not picking my nose. This sniffle is because of my allergies, folks. Don't make fun of me."

And, in discussing this with a friend, I discovered that I'm not alone in thinking that I'm not alone.

"I think my dog was a man in a previous life," she whispered.

"Why? Does he refuse to put the toilet seat down after he drinks?"

"Worse. He comes in the bedroom when I'm trying to change clothes and sits down to watch."

"What do you do?"

"Same thing I do with my husband. Put him out in the hall."

"Whenever my lights flicker, I think someone's trying to contact me from the other side," I admitted. "A couple of weeks ago, I thought they were trying to set up a family reunion. Then I realized it was just a power outage."

"Remember that movie where that little boy saw dead people all the time? Do you ever see dead people?"

"I'd say no, but you've seen my office at nine o'clock on Monday mornings."

She nodded in agreement. "Okay, what other ways do the dead visit us?"

"I hear some people say that people who have passed away come to them in their dreams. That one hasn't happened to me yet. Besides, they'd have to get through Mel, Keanu, Greg, Morten ..."

"Other relatives?"

"Fantasies."

"Oh." She thought for a moment. "For me, they'd have to come sit in my dream about the sixth grade final exam. And they'd have to be willing to be naked."

"Hope none of my relatives visit you. You wouldn't enjoy it."

So now, I have to feel guilty not only about forgetting to talk to my elderly relatives who are alive, but also about the ones who aren't.

Yes, now even when I'm alone, I'm self-conscious. Maybe I was better off thinking they were in the clouds.

✎ Hair Today, Gone Tomorrow

How times have changed. Just this week I heard my sister talking about her son's hair. It was awful, she moaned. She just couldn't believe it. He had gotten almost all of it cut off, even after she told him how much better it looked long. And even though the storyline was backward, I remembered a similar battle going on in my home some thirty-odd years ago.

It was disciplinary time. A juvenile misdeed had occurred. Mom and Dad stood before one of their children, saying, "We can't believe you did that. We are very upset with you."

The child nodded shamefully.

"You'll have to be punished."

The child nodded again.

"Okay, so which one are you? Martha Ann?"

The child shook its head vehemently.

"Wanda?"

No again.

"Christee?"

Three strikes, they were out of girls. I walked by just in time to solve the problem. "I think that's one of the boys, Mom."

"In that case, you'll not only get punished, you'll get a haircut, too."

The constant battle between parents and hair continues. And the battle doesn't end at hair—it carries over into clothing habits, too. I remember my rebellious days in high school.

"That's an unusual outfit. It reminds me of a bag lady I gave money to last week." Mom is known for her diplomacy, reminiscent of a Sherman tank.

"Yes, Mom, it's the latest style." I stood ready to defend my generation's garb.

"Why are your clothes torn? Did something happen to them?"

"That's the way they were when I bought them."

"Did you get them on sale because they were torn?"

"No, actually they were more expensive."

"I never wore clothes that were torn," she noted.

"Yes, but you also walked barefoot two hundred miles to school each day. Did you want me to be just like you in that situation, too?"

"It built character."

"It built calluses, Mom."

"But why would torn clothes be more expensive?"

"Because they're in style."

"Couldn't you just tear them yourself?"

"Oh, Mom. How embarrassing to have non-professionally torn clothes."

We kept on like this for some time. But she didn't win. I didn't change out of my torn outfit. Okay, she won a little. I did take off my shoes and walk to school that day.

Monday, April 30

✎ The Art of Conversation

While out of town on a business trip, I called home. I asked all the important questions, like, "How is the cat?" "Did I get a check from Ed McMahon?" and "Have you figured out what the furry green thing in the refrigerator is?" Then I remembered to ask, "And how are you, dear?"

This was about twelve minutes into the conversation. I discovered at this point that my husband had laryngitis. I didn't notice earlier because I seldom do those things that would allow my husband to speak, like breathe, pause, or ask his opinion.

I sometimes worry about the fact that I talk so much. In elevators when everyone is silent and staring at that silver door, I'm usually the one who speaks and says something reassuring like, "Wasn't there a scene in *The Towering Inferno* where the elevator plunged to the ground?"

Once, on an airplane, I talked to the man in the next seat nonstop from Nashville to Washington, D.C., and didn't realize until we were landing that the man was deaf. I had been wondering why he was the only person I ever visited with who continued to smile an hour into our conversation.

On that same trip, I carried on a great discussion with my cab driver, Churnet, from one of the –stan countries, like Pakistan or Uzbekistan. He didn't really have a command of the English language. After a ride through the city—twice—I discovered that Churnet didn't have a command of the city street system, either. Or maybe he was just a shrewd businessman.

I smile and speak to people on the streets. They check their pockets. I speak to animals. They pretend not to understand. I speak to people at work. They pretend not to understand, too.

And, unfortunately for my spouse, I wake up talking. A machine gun would probably be more pleasant in the early morning than me instantly jumping into a recounting of every dream from the night before.

"David, I can't believe you would do that to me," I said to him one morning immediately after waking up.

"Do what?"

"You ran out on me with another woman."

Shock, surprise, and horror showed up in his eyes. Well, it was either shock or a reaction from last night's experimental lasagna. "You were dreaming again, weren't you?" he finally asked.

"I'm not sure."

"What color was her hair?"

"Red."

"How could you do that to me? You know I'm not partial to redheads." But he was curious about his mystery woman, so he asked, "Was she attractive?"

"Not really."

"I really don't appreciate these dreams of yours. You could at least let me run off with somebody good-looking."

"It was my dream," I pouted.

He jumped on this. "Finally, I win. I actually win. You just admitted it was a dream."

Okay, this was a historic day. He actually won that round. But I got him back. The next night, I dreamed he ran off with another redhead.

✎ Three Little Words

Every so often I like to celebrate realizations I've had that make me happy. Today I had one of those. I realized that I love being middle-aged in the South. We have some of the most wonderful traditions—traditions that make life so much easier.

For example: We here in the South have a wonderful habit of being able to say anything we want to, about anyone, no matter how terrible it is, as long as we say three little words after it. No, not "I love you." Our three little words are "Bless her heart."

Let me show you how this works.

"Good Lord, that girl has gotten so big they're gonna have to give her a zip code. Bless her heart."

"That boy is so stupid. I think he's a brain cell shy of a turnip. Bless his heart."

Is this great or what? You can say terrible things; you just have to add the all-purpose disclaimer of "Bless her heart."

It could work in politics. Think how much more we would like politicians if they used it. Someone running for office could talk about his opponent, "He's a philanderer and a crook—nothing but a waste of space. Bless his heart."

Other customs in the South? How about the way we claim that unless people are from out of town, they aren't experts?

"Yes, we have this huge issue at the company that could result in our filing for bankruptcy. It could put hundreds of people out of work and result in our officers going to prison for ten to twenty. Fortunately, we have a consultant from Bogalusa coming in to work on the problem." And suddenly, everyone breathes a huge sigh of relief. As long as the expert is from farther than fifty miles away, everything is going to be okay.

Then there's that Southern tradition that isn't as much fun. The one that says we should spend at least one holiday a year with our family.

Like last Thanksgiving, when Mom, who is *not* known for her culinary expertise and *is* known for experimenting with unusual food combinations, created the first-known Turkey with Peanut Butter and Jelly Sauce. With an unparalleled side dish of sweet potato casserole that had something unusually crunchy in it, the meal was an interesting experience, to say the least.

Of course, the fact that she prepared it without setting off the smoke detector was a huge accomplishment. That Thanksgiving, Mom's cooking was rated as a major disaster, right behind the *Hindenberg*. Bless her heart.

✎ The Fat End of My Closet

Yes, I hate to go there. But it happens. Yesterday morning I was trying to zip up my pants and realized that somehow they had "shrunk" to a point that the only way that zipper was going up was if I cut the material on each side of it. Since that is frowned on in my office dress code, so I headed to that dark, dark place—the fat end of my closet.

"What's wrong?" David saw me staring into the back corner of my closet and spoke before thinking. Immediately he realized what I was looking at and tried to back out of the door. He was too slow.

"I'm fat. Why didn't you tell me I'm fat?"

This, of course, was one of those no-win questions. Like, "Do you beat your wife often?" and, "When did you realize that you were a loser?"

David just smiled and backed closer to the door.

"David, I'm enormous. I'm not sure I'll even fit into my fat clothes. What do I do?"

He really shouldn't have tried to answer this, but the man is much too accommodating. "You can wear something of mine."

I swooned. Yes, it is the one time in my life I truly swooned. A bald man of two hundred fifty pounds had offered me clothing. And there was the sobering moment when I considered it.

"No. This is it. I am going to exercise. I am going to get back down to the weight I was when we got married."

Pretty funny statement there. My feet alone now weigh what I weighed when we got married. I was a stick then. When you grow up in a family of six kids, all of whom are really fast eaters, you don't get fat. I wanted to be able to weigh enough to give blood back then. Now I'd like to give blood just to lose the pint of weight.

But after the zipper incident, I was determined. I got up early this morning, turned on one of those exercise shows, and sat down with my bottle of water to assess how to do the exercises. Twenty minutes later my husband entered the room.

"What a good idea. An exercise show."

"Yup."

"Are you going to sit and watch the whole thing?"

"Nope, I'm almost ready to join in."

"That's good." He pointed to the clock. "But this show is over in five minutes. That's not going to give you much of a workout."

"You can't rush into these things." Men, what do they know?

"Okay. Wouldn't want you to hurt yourself."

Thirty minutes later I was still sitting on the couch watching television. But now it was yoga. I was feeling very relaxed watching all those people breathing so deeply.

I wonder how long it will be before I feel safe watching high-impact aerobics.

✎ Cat Zen

I remember when I picked up my first book on Zen Buddhism. And then I found a book on Taoism. Then I read a few more books that outlined a number of other philosophies. I realized that they all had some interesting points, but they all said not to follow them, because their beliefs could not really be explained (like—*Strive with diligence, and be a lamp unto yourselves. – Buddha*—what the heck does that mean, anyway?). Their philosophies were experience-based.

In other words, by living you learn about Taoist thought. By being quiet and listening to your breathing, you're a step closer to Zen. Like they keep saying, if you can explain it, it just ain't it. Of course, that's my own very liberal translation.

So, where did all this study take me? Nowhere closer to where I thought I should be.

Then, today, as I was reading more books and making notes, MamaCat was becoming quite a distraction.

Allow me to introduce you. MamaCat is named so for the fact that she was a neighborhood stray who had litters of about fourteen kittens at a time. She is a huge, solid, black cat with a very composed attitude. Seventeen years old with an enormous stomach that swings back and forth like it's trying to hit opposite walls when she walks. And she's the most amazing cat I've ever met.

Anyway, during my study, MamaCat would shove her way into the middle of my papers every so often. She would plop down in the middle of everything and allow me to pet her for a few minutes. Then she would wander off in search of fresh amusements.

She would stare into space, totally amazed by the empty air in front of her. Then she would give her full and undivided attention to the licking of her paw. And then she would stare at me.

She wasn't trying to teach me anything, but in that moment, the moment when she stared so intently at me, she got a message through. I put down the book I was reading and stared back. We just sat there, staring at each other. Ignoring the phone when it rang. Breathing deeply. Experiencing this one moment. This here and now.

Cat Zen. Who'd have thunk it?

✎ A Leap and a Few Falls of Faith

I did it. I left my day job today. The thing they tell writers never to do. I am now like the old bra commercial—I have "no visible means of support."

I've spent so many years on the corporate ladder that I have calluses from hanging on for dear life. I've climbed up many rungs, fallen down a few rungs, and climbed right back up again. I changed ladders a number of times, which always puts you back down a few rungs. But now I was ready to leap off the ladder completely.

It was my leap of faith. I had been thinking about it for a long time, and I knew I was ready. I am dedicated to my writing career. I am scared to death.

Within two hours of leaving the office, panic set in.

"I won't get a paycheck next week?" I looked at my husband in shock.

"Not unless somebody pays you to eat," he laughed.

"Where do I apply?"

"It was a joke," he said gently.

"Now you write your own paycheck. You decide how big it is by hard work and determination."

"That's sick."

"No, that's exciting. You're the captain of your own ship."

"But they gave me money just to be the wine steward at the last ship," I moaned. "What have I done?"

"Taken a very exciting step toward controlling your future," he encouraged me.

"Yeah. Now I can focus on writing, my books, my speaking engagements," I listed.

"That's more like it."

"And my bills, my need for health insurance, my dwindling account balance."

"Okay, we've gone astray again," he noted.

"It's just scary. But if you're not scared, you're not trying anything new, right?"

He nodded.

"And if you don't try anything new, you'll never know what you could have achieved, right?"

He nodded again, more vigorously this time.

"And a life without trying to achieve goals and using the talents you have been given is a life wasted, right?"

He nodded even more, then applauded and grinned from ear to ear.

"And if it doesn't work, I can always be a telemarketer, right?"

He nodded off to sleep. He'd heard this rationale before.

Yes, I'm thrilled to have left the security of a nine-to-five job to leap into a world of boundless possibilities. Yes, I realize that if I don't make it, I no longer have anyone else to blame. And yes, I know that I will be looking at the classifieds every time I have a bad week.

Yes, I'm taking an exciting leap of faith. Now if I can just step away from the safety net.

✎ Happy Anniversaries and Sad Goodbyes

My husband and I celebrated our anniversary today. It always takes me back to the most important day of my life— next to the one when I discovered a hair growing from my armpit. My wedding day. It was ... interesting.

All that morning I was in a state of shock. I wasn't worried about being married. I wasn't worried about the honeymoon. I was worried that everyone in that church knew that I was going to be a *naughty* girl that night.

I'd spent twenty-three years saying "no" and now in one day a priest would mumble a few phrases and I would have to start saying "yes," or at least, "I have a headache." It wasn't frightening; it was confusing.

Even all these years later, I still remember quite a few things about the wedding and the honeymoon. I remember my father whispering as we walked down the aisle, "There's the side door. We can still make a run for it."

When I walked by our families at the front of the aisle, I remember seeing my entire family grinning from ear to ear and his whole family crying. I might have been insulted here. I wasn't sure.

I remember talking to the Bishop just before the ceremony. Unfortunately we couldn't understand him very well due to a respiratory problem. So we just smiled and laughed in the pauses he left. Later, I found out he had been talking about his deceased parents.

I remember climbing into a Toyota in a hoop skirt to go to the reception. I don't remember much about the drive. Though all I could see was a huge white skirt pushing up over the dashboard, I do remember hearing cheers from the gas station attendants.

I remember a reception that was unconventional. It was a crawfish boil and we refused to leave until we had eaten as many crawfish as we could hold. We were actually the last guests to leave.

I remember our honeymoon to Six Flags Over Texas. A sudden cold spell had settled in and we discovered how packing a week's worth of shorts for a summer vacation that turned into a cold front could be a problem.

And I remember having to end our honeymoon early due to a death in my new family. We rushed back to New Orleans for Aunt Billie's funeral.

As I watched Uncle Cliff break down by the casket, crying, I realized what it was really all about. We'd had the perfect wedding. We'd had the fun. And now we had been brought back down to Earth. If I had been Uncle Cliff, I think I would have died at the loss of my soul mate. He did, a few months later.

✎ I Fought the Lawn, and the Lawn Won

The scariest sound in the world. It's not a chainsaw revving up in the hands of a ski-masked man. It's not the rattle of the back door when you're home alone.

No. The scariest sound in the world is the one that woke me up this morning. It's the sound of the next-door neighbor yanking his lawnmower into action at seven o'clock on a Saturday morning when you know that your grass is nearing the bottom of the windows on your house. You can almost hear your grass growing as this inconsiderate piece of humanity who retired at fifty-five putters around on his jumbo riding tractor that takes about two swipes to finish the entire yard.

So, now your grass looks even taller. You know that somewhere under the grass line you have a small dog living in the backyard. Then the neighbor begins to compound the injury by edging, weed-eating, shaping, and then blowing the grass into your yard. Action must be taken.

I put on my sexy pair of shorts. The ones with one pocket that hangs lower than the shorts themselves. The ones that were in style when Ford was falling around the White House. I tried to start the lawnmower.

Half an hour later, my arm was sore, my temper was flaring, and my mate was completely amused.

"Having trouble?"

"No. It's a new aerobic workout," I said, shrugging. "Or maybe the lawnmower's just cold."

"It's smoking."

"Well, it might have warmed up a little."

"Want me to start it for you?" he offered.

"No. I can do it myself."

"I wouldn't mind."

"I really don't need any help. Thank you."

"Have you checked everything on it?"

"What is there to check? It's a lawnmower. This is a lawn. The rest should be easy."

"Well, it *is* an old mower," he gently rationalized.

"You think just because I'm a woman I can't do this. You think women are not mechanically inclined. You think that I've forgotten to check all the silly little details. Well, let me tell you something. I was cutting an acre-yard when I was barely tall enough to see over the lawnmower handlebars. I know these machines. And I'm in great shape. So don't try talking down to me."

Okay, actually he wasn't. Actually we get along very well. I just get a tad frustrated when machinery won't work for me.

"You're upset," he noted.

"Well, yes. We have a maintenance contract on this machine so that this sort of thing won't happen."

"I know what you mean." He was so understanding. "Look, don't let it upset you. I'll take the thing in tomorrow and get it checked. It's probably something minor."

"I hope so," I mumbled angrily.

"Don't worry about it."

"Okay."

"Guess I'll go watch baseball on TV," David decided.

"Yeah." I smiled. "Guess I'll go try to find a spot where the weeds don't overshadow me too much so I can sunbathe."

I was soothed. Everything was all right. Except for the little thing I noticed as I wheeled that ridiculous red machine back to the garage. The fuel tank was empty.

✎ Dumb Animals? How Often Do You Get Free Meals for Sleeping?

We have pets. No children. Children require clothes, schooling, and attention. My pets require nothing—nothing except gourmet food, the dining room table for their bed, our legs for scratching posts, and constant petting.

They never use four-letter words. They make their own amusement. My cat particularly enjoys dust bunnies. Being the wonderful mother I am, I leave lots of them around the house for her amusement. And my dog is brain-dead. She spent yesterday morning fighting her shadow. The shadow won.

This morning I had one of those early morning wrong number phone calls. I knew I wasn't going back to sleep, so I got up and did what anyone would do at three o'clock in the morning. I cleaned the closet in the guest bedroom. I was relatively pleased. There was nothing alive in there. My cat watched the process with interest.

"What's your problem?"

"Meow."

"Give me a break. I don't understand Cat Latin."

The feline was not amused. "Meow."

"You're hungry?" Yes, if cat food has been sitting out longer than 27.5 minutes, my pet feels it is not fresh enough to eat. So I tripped toward the kitchen. I opened a new can of the latest gourmet seafood feast. It smelled better than what I cooked for supper last night. I plopped the whole can on her dish. She stared at me.

"Meow."

"Not hungry? Need to go out?" I opened the back door, where her yard-wide litter box awaited. She backed away from it.

"Not outside?" I was now running out of possibilities.

"Meow."

I was getting perturbed. "You want petting? That must be it."

I pulled her into my lap and stroked her head indifferently. She purred for a moment, like a car deciding whether to start. Then she pulled away.

She jumped to the floor. "Meow."

At this point I was getting desperate. "What do you want? A toy?" I gave her a couple of her pet dust bunnies. She was not interested.

I pulled out more toys from the closet. I found yarn in a drawer. I put a pillow on the floor for her. I turned on the radio to her favorite music. I turned on the television to the *Animal Planet*. I gave her a couple of my husband's socks.

Pretty soon the room looked like a tornado had hit. And what did MamaCat say?

"Meow."

I screamed, ran to the bedroom, and threw myself back into bed, where my husband was just stirring. He yawned, stretched, and opened one glazed eye toward the alarm clock. He turned over and smiled at me with that endearing, loving smile that I live for.

He chirped, "Just about time to get up. I'll make coffee." He jumped up, refreshed from a night of deep sleep, and headed for the kitchen. The cat took his place in the bed.

"Meow." She curled herself into a little ball and purred herself to sleep in his spot.

Next time I'll let him answer the phone.

✎ Dumb Animals Part Two

My pets are a constant source of embarrassment.

My cat's favorite toy is the dust bunny, but of course she never pulls one out to play with unless there's company in the house. She'll go grab one out from under the bed, preferably with a mummified insect enclosed and parade it in front of our visitors. She also has a problem with flatulence.

My bird, Elvis, loves to scream so the neighbors worry about what is going on in our house. When I get on the phone, she gets jealous and curses. I punish her when she's been bad by eating fried chicken in front of her.

At one point, I was president of a humane society. I had thirteen cats, two dogs, and a parrot living under one roof. It was ugly. No one ever came to visit. Especially since we tried to sneak an animal into their purse or car before they left.

About a week ago I actually tried to entertain. My parents came over for supper. I cooked spaghetti. Everything was going well. We adjourned to the living room for coffee. Mother admired our dog, Narlee.

"What a cute pup."

"Yes," I agreed, "but she is a little hyperactive. She gets really excited over any attention."

"How can you tell?" Mom asked, and Narlee proceeded to show her by having an accident on her leg. "It's all right," she answered, in that comforting tone that our mothers' generation has.

But it wasn't all right. I could see the cat working her way toward Mom, with her tail straight up in the air—a sure sign that *wind* was about to come. "Shall we go to the backyard?" I suggested quickly, but not quickly enough.

"Oh look, it's your cat," Mom picked her up and squeezed her gently in her arms. Bad move. Mom's face registered shock.

"Honey!" She poked Daddy.

"No, Mom, it's not Daddy. The cat has a little stomach problem."

She placed the cat gingerly on the floor. About this time we saw that the parrot was stalking her. Elvis has this gait resembling the Hunchback of Notre Dame. Mother picked up her purse, which the dog had been chewing on, and grabbed Dad's arm.

"I think it's time to go home."

They ran out of the door. They will probably never come to visit again. It's really a shame. I wanted them to meet my iguana.

✎ The Joy of Shopping

I can't tell you how many times I've gone window shopping, stopped while looking at some display with a mannequin in a pose that is not humanly possible, and said, "I can't afford to buy anything, so why am I shopping?"

Then, while the people around me are trying to figure out what invisible person the crazy woman is talking to, I pick myself up and go home to cut up my plastic before the urge strikes again.

We Americans are obsessed with the idea of living above our incomes. We can't afford to eat foods from all four food groups, but we'll buy a videocassette recorder to record shows that we wouldn't watch even if we did have the time.

We can go shopping at the same store three times in one week. Do we think that they restock this quickly? No. Do we think our tastes might have changed in this period? No. Do we think things might look different to us at another time of day? No.

We are just waiting for the point of desperation to arrive when the urge to "buy something" becomes so great that even the green-and-orange-plaid cargo vest looks good to us. I personally believe that average Americans spend anywhere from one-third to three-thirds of their lives chasing blue lights.

And, of course, when you talk about shopping, you have to talk about garage sales. This is that great American phenomenon where you go to someone's home and, contrary to the name, do not get to buy a garage at all, but instead a huge quantity of someone else's junk from their closets that you will promptly take home and put in your closets.

I must admit, that I, too, have fallen prey. And my husband is my witness. I came face to face with him this afternoon as I snuck in through the back door. "You've been to another garage sale, haven't you?"

"What makes you think that?" I asked defensively, the somewhat mildewed moose head sticking out from behind my back.

"Why do you do this to yourself?"

"Someday, the world's greatest bargain could be waiting for me at a garage sale. If I miss it, there'll never be a second chance."

"Sure there will be. The person who bought it will get tired of it, put it in their garage sale, and then you can buy it."

"You think I just buy useless junk at these things, don't you?" I couldn't believe he didn't understand the complexity of these events.

"Well, I could be influenced. Show me what you bought today."

I held out my prizes like a child with a crayon drawing. There was the moose head, from which one antler had become dislodged. There was a size twenty-two maternity dress. Sure, we never plan to have children, but I thought it would be a safe addition to the fat end of my closet. And somehow, there was a small child behind my back.

"Who are you?" I was a little confused.

"Cindy."

"And where did I pick you up?"

"Palm Street."

"How much did I pay for you?"

"Seventy-five cents."

"There you have it," I shouted to my husband. "Proof positive of how valuable these events are. If we had gotten her through that hospital route, she'd have cost thousands!"

He made me take Cindy back. It's okay though—I traded her in for a kitten.

Garage sales—because one's man's trash will soon become another man's trash.

✎ A Rubber Chicken in Every Boardroom

To earn a little extra cash, I taught a session today on "Humor in the Workplace" and, as usual, I took my rubber chicken with me (Please don't ask why I carry a rubber chicken with me—it's a religious thing). It reminded me of the old saying, "A chicken in every pot." That saying was about sharing the wealth. It was about being sure every person had something. It was not very useful to vegetarians. But it was a good maxim when you think about the concept of humor.

Some people seem to think laughter should be reserved for appropriate venues like comedy clubs, humorous movies, opposing parties' political speeches, and situation comedies.

But I remember the first time I realized that humor could be a valuable tool in the high-powered world of executives and corporations.

I was seated at the conference table in a company boardroom, in the middle of one of the most negative meetings I had ever experienced. I looked around and saw severe faces, all framed by ties in the latest power color. I saw the smug face of the fellow who had managed to capture the "power seat" next to the president. And I was listening to the "sniper" of the group who was throwing out yet another reason that the latest plan wouldn't work.

I threw my rubber chicken at him.

A moment of shocked silence ensued.

"And this means?" He held up the offending creature by one limp yellow leg.

"You said something negative. Now you're stuck with the chicken until someone else says something negative."

"What?" The puckered look on his face was less than enthusiastic. Or maybe that was the reaction from the Thai lunch that he had just devoured in under six minutes.

"Don't worry," I reassured him. "You're just holding the chicken until the next negative remark. At the rate this meeting has been going, you won't have him long."

"What a stupid idea," Joe piped up.

"See what I mean?" I winked at John, the sniper.

He caught my meaning. He actually laughed, which no one had seen John do since the Reagan years. He reared back and flung the chicken at Joe, who sat shocked into silence. This was actually quite a nice change for Joe.

And that was the beginning. It was at this moment that I realized that humor could be a tool for good and not evil. I realized that it could make a point—and humor in the boardroom was actually safer than on the stage at comedy clubs, where people were quicker to make dangerous projectiles out of innocent, but often surprisingly sharp, items.

That was when I realized what my true career should be—I should be a humor consultant (Definition: a person who can't hold a job in business or comedy clubs).

We all have our missions. Mine is apparently to keep the rubber chicken industry in business. I'd like to think it's more important than that, but I'll settle for small steps.

✎ My Indian Name: Dances With Worries

Yesterday, my husband and I were driving down a little side street in our neighborhood when I spotted a big orange cat sitting on the roof of a house.

"David!" I screeched. I tend to screech in crisis situations. "We have to call the fire department."

"Where's the fire?" He careened to the side of the road, prepared to jump out and save anyone and anything, provided that it wasn't too heavy or scratchy.

"No, it's even worse." I pointed a trembling hand toward the cat that, at that very moment, yawned and curled into a ball, evidence of its terror-stricken state.

David assessed the situation and shrugged, "Maybe we should just tell the owner."

"Well, I suppose that would be one option."

No one was home. Or maybe they were home and just afraid of the strange woman standing at their door, yelling, "Here kitty, kitty!" for no obvious reason.

"I'd better just climb up and get him down," I said.

"I don't think that's a good idea," David patted me on the shoulder. I could tell he was remembering the last time I got on anything higher than a step stool. The people at the hospital didn't understand how anyone could break a limb by falling less than ten inches.

"How about the fire department?" I suggested again, and before he could even answer, a shocking realization hit me.

"David, in all my forty-plus years of life, I have never once seen a dead cat on a roof."

Now, I know that all cats that get up on roofs are not rescued by people calling 911. And yet, somehow they must make it down from there. Otherwise we would be seeing little cat bodies on rooftops all over town.

David added, "You know, I've never seen a cat skeleton in a tree either."

We stared at each other in complete shock.

Entire television episodes have been built on the storyline of a cat up a tree. Our hardy firemen have spent time and effort climbing trees to rescue cats that, it suddenly appeared, did not need rescuing.

I have been involved in humane societies, so it's not that I was underestimating the importance of cats. And it was not that I'm inconsiderate toward cats—as my twenty-pound former stray will attest. She eats at two-hour intervals during the night. On the other hand, if my husband asks for as much as a glass of water at night, I laugh myself to sleep over his request.

But in that moment I realized how much I overestimate my importance in the scheme of things. I worry about things that I really don't need to worry about. I think I have to watch over the world. And I end up with the beginning of ulcers, stress disorders, and lots of extra gray hairs for my trouble.

So this time, I left it to a power even higher than the fire department.

Today, when I drove by, the cat was busy playing with a leaf in the front yard of the house.

✎ Man's Best Friend

I am embarrassed about our dog, Narlee. She has no social graces, no pedigree, and unfortunately, no brain. But she does have a personality.

Originally, Narlee's name was spelled "Gnarly." We thought it was a cute combination of our former home in Los Angeles and the fact that she chewed on everything in sight. Then her name was shortened, dropping that silent G, making her name Narly. But then today, the dog apparently developed an attitude (just like the planet Uranus, which suddenly decided it didn't like the pronunciation of its name) and she insisted that we spell her name like her mom's—with two e's at the end.

I came home to find a note on the door that said, "Did you bring at me some bones? Signed, Narlee."

I was not as shocked that Narlee had learned to write or had changed the spelling of her name as much as I was over-whelmed that Narlee had such a bad command of the use of prepositions. I should have expected that, though. Narlee is just plain stupid.

Now I don't say this without proof. Let us consider the fact that Narlee insists on warning the neighbors that I am home each evening. Let a large man in a ski mask with a bloody axe enter our yard and Narlee is the welcoming committee, begging for a Purina Snausage. But when I come home, Narlee feels it is her duty to bark until she nearly rebates her dinner.

Of course, Narlee knows that she alone can protect the world from that vicious creature—the killer squirrel. She will bark until she has no voice left to warn us that the man-eating squirrel is in the general vicinity. The only thing that can quiet her at this point is if the large man in the ski mask reassures her that the squirrel is no threat.

For the first few years we had Narlee, she had an annual rash on her stomach. We took her to vet after vet. And, when those war heroes proved to be of no use, we took her to a veterinarian. Still, no answer. We finally just accepted that Narlee had some strange rash that could not be understood.

Then, one bright summer day, I looked out of the kitchen window to discover Narlee, lying on her back, legs spread wide apart in a most unladylike position. And on her stomach the red rash was getting redder. Narlee's mysterious rash was none other than a sunburn. I don't believe this is supposed to be possible for dogs, but once I got her to consider using a higher level of sunscreen, the rash disappeared.

✎ More of Man's Best Friend

Narlee loves cats. She wants to be buddies with MamaCat, our black cat who is approximately the size of a Volkswagen and who possesses the amiability of Genghis Khan. Narlee wants to play. MamaCat wants doggie for a snack. The two have found a compromise. MamaCat doesn't remove any vital organs from Narlee as long as Narlee doesn't breathe near MamaCat.

But despite her lack of a brain, Narlee does have as gentle and sweet a disposition as anyone's could be. During the flood of '87, I remember how David and I waded through twelve inches of water in the house, then dashed outdoors into the flood to find Narlee. There she was, perched on the highest piece of furniture she could find in our utility shed. Sitting next to her was her new best friend, a field mouse. It would have made a beautiful picture. Just the two of them against the flood. And, of course, they were both barking at the killer squirrel.

✎ A Girl Named Emma, Mangoes, and True Love

I know this shows that, with age, my patience is wearing thin, but since this is the second time this has happened, I just have to ask the question: Why do people always call wrong numbers at three o'clock in the morning? If I were going to call someone at that time of day, I'd make darn sure that I had the right number. And who are all these people calling each other at that time of day? It makes me feel like there's a whole world of excitement in the wee morning hours that I'm missing out on.

Nevertheless, when it happened—again—this morning, I kicked a few animals out of the way and stumbled across the penetrating cold of the floor to the screeching phone.

"Hello." A few more appropriate words came to mind, but this one had to suffice for the moment.

"Is Emma there?"

"No. Nobody by that name here."

"Where is she?"

"Beats me. She doesn't live here."

"Where does she live?"

"I have no idea."

"So, Emma's not home?"

"She might be."

"Could I speak to her then?"

"She's not here." Okay, at this point it was starting to feel like a new version of *Who's on First!*

"When will she be back?"

"She won't be back. Emma doesn't live here."

"How long have you had this number?"

I was tired by this point, so you'll have to forgive my response. "Ever since Emma died and left it to me in her will."

Silence.

That was a pleasant moment, but too short-lived. He continued, "Emma's dead?"

"Yes, freak mango accident."

"So, I don't have a date with her on Friday?"

"Guess not."

"What are you doing Friday?"

"Visiting Emma."

I hung up the phone. This conversation was pointless. I had plans for Friday night.

So, Emma was one of those three o'clock in the morning party girls and I had just ruined her Friday. I could imagine her waiting for her prince, perhaps with a bowl of mangoes by the door. I felt somewhat guilty, but mostly I just felt sleepy.

I fell onto the bed, ready to be engulfed back into that great dream where Greg Kinnear sees me in the audience during the taping of a David Letterman show. He leaves the stage and runs to me in the audience, arms outstretched, that gorgeous smile lighting up his face. It's always in slow motion. Lasts longer like that. Sexual tension is my favorite pastime.

But once I was draped across the bed again, ready for my dream, my husband turned over and those airplane engines started up.

"Honey," (we always use those cutesy names when we're talking to each other) "you're snoring again."

"No, I'm not," he mumbled into his pillow.

"Yes, you are."

"You're dreaming."

"No, Mr. Kinnear was not snoring. You were."

He knows about my Greg Kinnear fixation. He was not amused, especially in the middle of the night.

"I don't snore."

"Oh, I forgot." I rolled him over and he stopped snoring, or possibly breathing. I was so tired, I wasn't sure I cared.

I finally got back to my dream of Greg Kinnear. He was running up to me in the Letterman audience. He was getting closer and closer. Then he was right there in front of me. That beautiful sandy golden hair. That wonderful dimple. His arms were stretched out toward me. And then he passed me up and ran to Emma in the row behind me.

✎ Sunshine on My Shoulders and Neighbors at My Fence

I decided to sunbathe in my backyard, assuming that this way, I would have some privacy, as opposed to going out on a beach where children would snicker and point at the woman with the pudgy tummy, while seafaring types would try to roll me back out to sea. I was wrong about this assumption.

As soon as I got comfortable on my oldest towel, the one with the parrot droppings mixed in with the psychedelic colors, my neighbor felt impelled to walk into his backyard and speak to me.

"Going to try to get some sun, eh?"

Obviously that PhD in action. "Yes." I thought a short answer would discourage the man from continuing the conversation. I was wrong.

He pushed back his greasy black hair and looked upward to the sky. "Could rain."

There was not a cloud in the sky. His PhD was obviously not in meteorology.

"Hmmm." I thought perhaps this even shorter, more nondescript answer would give him the message. Wrong again.

The old codger was leaning on my hurricane fence, leering. I didn't understand. There was nothing to leer at. I wasn't even wearing a revealing bathing suit. It was one of those "I borrowed this from mom because I'm too fat to wear any of mine" bathing suits. But he seemed to be enjoying himself.

The party continued. His sons came out and propped themselves up on the fence. "Hi, Mrs. Atwood."

Great. What was this—sex education on a budget? I could just imagine him saying to his boys, "See sons, this is what women look like when they go to pot. That's why I make your mother stay inside. She was getting that round stomach and those blue squiggly lines on her legs, too. Ain't a pretty sight, is it?"

Then, when I thought it couldn't get worse, visitors drove up to his house. At first I was greatly relieved. I thought that finally they would go inside and leave me to my sun worshipping. Instead the visitors joined them at the fence.

"These are my friends from the plant," he thought it necessary to inform me. I looked up to discover seven men with approximately twenty teeth between them.

"Hello." I opened my romance book and began to feign interest.

"You trying to get a tan?" One of the men joined in this scintillating conversation.

I politely answered, "Yes." And I tried to pretend that I was sleepy. I exaggerated a yawn and placed the book over my face.

"Got a book, huh?"

"Yes." How could I argue with their keen powers of observation?

For a while the men lingered, but as their discussion of work moved on to tasty subjects like the proper gutting of deer and the directional spitting of tobacco, they seemed to lose interest in me.

Finally they turned and headed into the house, the promise of beer and belches awaiting them. Once again, it was just the sun, my backyard, and me.

I turned over, positioned myself perfectly on my towel for maximum exposure, took a sip of lemonade, and perched my sunglasses back up on my nose. Applying a little of my deliciously greasy cocoa butter to my legs, I took a deep breath, inhaling the intoxicating scent of honeysuckle and freshly cut grass.

And then the rain started.

✎ Mr. Communication and Miscommunication

Last night as my husband slept next to me, I just stared at him. We have this problem—we like each other. In this day and age of colorful marital arguments on *Jerry Springer*, I have a husband who never fights. He accepts the fact that I'm an expert on everything. This means we never get to go to a marriage counselor and I never have nasty stuff to complain to my friends about. The man is ruining my life.

This morning, I decided to approach him about this problem.

"David, we never fight."

"So?"

"Well, we must not care about each other very much if we don't fight."

"Oh?"

"Yeah. Fighting is supposed to be a way of communicating. If we don't do it, then we must be out of touch with each other."

"Maybe we just agree on the basic concepts of life."

"Don't be silly."

"Well," he became serious, "what do you think we should do about this problem?"

"Aha! So you agree that we have a problem!"

"If you say we have a problem, we must."

"See, there you go again!" I screeched. "You always agree with me. You won't fight."

"What do you want me to do? Disagree with you just to start a fight?"

"Now that's silly."

"Okay, I'm open to suggestions. What do you want me to do?"

"Quit being so cooperative. Tell me how you really feel."

"I really feel like we don't have a problem."

"So you disagree with me."

"I guess so."

"So, what you're saying is," I thought back to the interpersonal communication research paper that I made a C on in my college psychology class, "that I'm being stupid and ridiculous."

"No."

"Then you're saying that you hate the way I make mashed potatoes."

"You never make mashed potatoes."

"Aha! So that's the problem!"

"I'm allergic to potatoes."

"It's probably a psychological allergy. You probably just think I'm not as good a cook as your mother."

"Well, we've always agreed on that. You hate to cook."

"So you're saying that our lack of communication is because of my lack of domestic ability."

"No."

"Stop arguing with me. You know I'm right."

"Okay."

"What do you mean by that?"

"I don't know. What is 'okay' supposed to mean?"

"Oh, so now you're getting sarcastic. How dare you throw my cooking in my face like that? How dare you talk to me like this?"

"I'm sorry."

"Well, you should be."

He left the room. He had lost the fight. And I felt much better. As long as we can communicate like this, there is still hope for our marriage.

✎ If I Could Do That, I Wouldn't Need a Health Club

Now here's a scary concept—me in a health club.

I decided to go try out a health club this week. All in all, the experience was not pretty.

I can't understand why I get this macho desire in a health club to hide the fact that I am in extreme pain with every exercise I try. I am a dainty little female. Well, I'm female. It shouldn't bother me to let others see that I am not as strong as a pack mule. But when I go to the health club, I have to row this stupid little boat twenty miles. Then I jump up and try to walk with knees that are heading for separate polar caps.

"This machine is for your triceps." This from a little girl in neon tights who looks anorexic, has sun-streaked blonde hair, and a tan with no visible tan lines that tells me she never mows her own yard—or she does so in the nude.

"Why do I want to build up my triceps?"

"Well, you want to build up all of your body."

"But are my triceps really all that useful? I mean, will they help me type faster?"

"You do want a complete workout, don't you?"

"Well, I thought I did. But this triceps thing is uncomfortable. Why don't we just leave well enough alone for the old triceps?"

"We'll try some other machines." She walked off, confused. I had a feeling that I had messed up her routine and she had forgotten the rest of her lines.

The next machine the girl led me to had me pulling down bicycle handlebars with weights on them. I was to lower them gently, without letting them touch the rest of the weights, and then lift them again. That's tricky when the weights are behind you. How are you supposed to see if the weights are about to touch until you hear that huge metallic clunk that tells you they already touched? I complained of a crick in my neck on the second try and she suggested we move on.

"This one is for your thighs."

I looked long and hard at these weights that I was to yank inward with my legs. I remembered that my mother had told me never to sit in that position in public. "Pass."

Then I discovered that another trainer was going to lead me through the rest of the machines. On first sight, I knew I had it made. He looked like Jody from *Family Affair*. I just knew I could pull the old "I'm just a weak little girl" routine and snow this guy easily. But after his first words, I knew I was wrong. I had encountered the Trainer from Hell.

"Okay, we'll go through all the machines. Then I want you to go back and do three sets on each."

I looked around the room at the assorted instruments of torture. I thought I could do it. But within ten minutes I had fallen off a treadmill, had a bicycle tell me that if I didn't pedal faster it would shut off, and gotten stranded on the second floor with a stair-step machine.

Totally disgusted, Jody gave me back to Miss Perfect Tan.

By the time we had finished going around the room, she had discovered the only thing I could do was to perch on the exercise bike, since that at least allowed me to sit down comfortably.

She left me on the bike for the rest of my visit with a health shake in one hand, a romance book in the other, and a television in front of me. I felt pretty healthy. Next week when I go in, I'll try pedaling.

✎ Sayings, Signs, and Other Mysteries

Today a woman walked by me and said, "How's it going?" By the time I replied, "I think I have the bubonic plague," she was already out of sight.

It fascinates me that we spend 99.9 percent of our lives saying things that we have memorized as common courtesies. Or is that the pureness of Ivory soap? Whatever the case, every day we say things like, "How are you?" I've heard this said to people in traction whose homes have just burnt down. And they answer with that other common courtesy, "Fine, thank you."

Something's just a little wrong here. I think if we cataloged all the useless, trite, or otherwise confusing things we say each day, we would be more than a trifle embarrassed.

"Opposites attract." I personally think this is the most ridiculous line since, "Thank God we have a Republican in office. Everything will be all right now."

"Eat all of that. There are children starving in India." So where are they when I need someone to take this hideous broccoli off my hands?

"It's all for the best." This actually translates to, "Something horrible just happened. I'm mad as heck and I must rationalize it or kill something."

Rubberneckers shake their bouncy little heads and cluck, "What a bad place for an accident." Does this mean there's a good place?

"You never miss it until it's gone." Boy, how true. I should have started missing it while I still had it.

Signs also amaze me. Apparently we have a desire to keep sign companies open at all costs, so we create a need for signs that are virtually useless. When driving down the highway, what do we see?

"Slippery when wet." Surprise, Einstein. Most things are. And they draw these little lines that look like snakes chasing a car. Great. Now the illiterates on the road think this is a snake zone.

"Bridge may ice in cold weather." I live in Louisiana. If it ever gets that cold, chances are we know that ice is pretty much a possibility. And seeing these signs in the sweltering heat of summer just depresses me. There's enough to depress me without seeing an unnecessary sign.

"Seeing-eye dogs allowed." So, we have a visually impaired person standing in front of a door. We have a dog standing next to this person. And we have a sign painted on the door that says, "Seeing-eye dogs allowed." Does anybody besides me see the problem here?

"Deer crossing." How do deer know where they're supposed to cross? I've never seen a deer standing at one of these signs waiting to cross. They usually cross the road wherever they want to. Whether that's because of the high rate of illiteracy among deer or because deer have serious attitude problems and think they are above the law, I just don't know.

The world's greatest sign? It is painted on the side of bank cars. "No cash carried in this vehicle." Now, is this chicken or what? They have this painted on the car, a kid in a baseball cap driving, and in the McDonald's bag on the back seat, there's a couple of hundred grand.

And, of course, Mr. Would-Be Thief is on the side of the road saying to his partner, "Well Elvin, it says, 'No cash carried in this vehicle,' and they wouldn't lie about a thing like that." So who needs armored cars?

Let's carry this further. Planes flying across the border could have painted on the side, "No drugs carried on this plane." Undercover police could sit in cars with signs that say, "No cops in this car." This is it. The world's greatest scam.

"After dark, store has less than $30." So, apparently nobody shops at this store at night. They obviously need a good advertising campaign more than they need another sign.

"The end." We see this sign at the end of every movie, but we know better. There's always a sequel.

✎ Seeing One's Feet: A Highly Overrated Pastime

Last week I looked down and realized I hadn't seen my feet in a while. They were hiding under a stomach that used to be reasonably flat and unobtrusive. Now that same stomach was competing with my chest to see which could stick out the farthest. Time for another diet.

It used to be that my cooking was bad enough that I kept a pretty slim figure. But unfortunately, I married a man who can cook. We'd both tried diets in the past, and we decided to go through the list to see which one would work again.

"Dolly Parton diet?" he suggested.

This was an interesting 'chemical' diet, which had us eating only eggs for one day, only bananas the next, and so on. This one had its good side. We stayed semi-conscious the entire time and didn't realize how sick we felt. However, the bad side—that silly habit of passing out on stairs—won out and we gave up on the Dolly Parton diet. Besides, I'd heard she couldn't see her feet either.

"Next," I suggested. "How about the water diet?"

I liked this one. It involved less cooking. You drank tons of water before each meal and as a snack, too. Not extremely tasty, but filling. The problem occurred in traveling from place to place. You found yourself becoming agoraphobic for an unusual reason. It was the fear of being in a wide-open space that had no bathroom. Trips to other cities were out of the question. The most important thing you asked before you went to visit people was, "How many bathrooms do you have?" But the upside was that you didn't have time to think about food, as you were always in a hurry to find the next bathroom. But for some reason, the appeal of this diet waned. We found ourselves searching for yet another way to slimness.

"What about one of those organized diets?"

"You mean *pay* to lose weight?" I was shocked.

"Yeah. You know, eat their food in their proportions and lose weight."

"Sounds scary."

But we decided to try it out. At the weight loss center, the red-haired woman with the fixed plastic smile looked us up and down and almost lost her composure. "Do we exercise?" she asked with her best royal 'we.' She should have known better.

"Exercise?" I looked at my husband in bewilderment.

"Yeah, you know, jumping around and all that," he refreshed my memory.

"Exercise?" I parroted.

"Do we exercise?" She repeated the question.

"I don't know about you, but we don't," I admitted.

"None?"

"Well," I thought hard, and she looked hopeful. "I did walk down the driveway to the mailbox last week instead of driving."

My husband beamed. "And me, I ran from the couch to the refrigerator at breaks in the game this weekend."

The woman was looking decidedly nervous. "What about our eating habits? What times do we eat?"

"Whenever the guy gets there with the pizza," my husband said, and I nodded in agreement.

"Let's write down everything you ate yesterday," she suggested as a starting point.

Two hours later we were still adding the cheese microwave popcorn and brownies to the list when she finally stopped us. "This is enough," she broke down. "I can't believe you ate all this. You were sent here by another weight loss center to drive us crazy, weren't you?"

My husband and I knew this was not a good sign. We spoke sincerely to the woman for another hour, but when we left, she still had not given us their diet food. In fact, we left with lollipops.

✎ A Hobby a Day

For the most part, I only partake of hobbies that I believe will someday be profitable to me. Usually these hobbies just end up costing me money. Like today, when getting rid of the evidence of an old hobby cost me the price of a classified ad. This was not the first time I've gotten caught up in a hobby, however. Before I got to this point, I had a long string of hobbies over the years.

There was photography. I bought a foreign camera. I bought a zoom lens to shoot pictures of people with bad breath and a wide-angle lens in case I ever had the opportunity to photograph Sumo wrestlers in action.

I bought filters that created stars, rainbows, and unnatural blue shades in faces. I bought attachments and a camera case so enormous that it needed wheels. I read books on photography and studied other photographers' work. I took two and one half rolls of film. They didn't look like those other photographers' pictures.

Other people had pictures of rare birds, special events, and candid facial expressions. I had pictures of branches where rare birds had been sitting only moments before, the clean up crews at special events, and my nephew sticking his tongue out at me.

The last roll of film I took was in 1990. It's still in the camera.

And so I moved on. One day I was sketching with a broken piece of pencil I found in the bottom of my purse. I discovered a previously unknown ability to sketch faces. The drawings were actually quite good, according to an art teacher.

Encouraged, I bought a drawing pad, charcoals, assorted drawing tools, and a dozen books on the subject of drawing.

I sat down to draw again. I sketched a few faces. Now that I had all the right equipment, the pictures stunk. I tried drawing a landscape. The tree looked like a snake with rigor mortis. I tried caricatures. They looked more like those trees I had been trying to draw. I put my drawings aside. They have stayed aside for ten years now.

And then, a few years ago, I decided to delve into a hobby I had never considered before—physical fitness. My husband flinched.

"What equipment are you going to buy?"

"I'm hurt that you would ask such a question. I don't need equipment. I've got this book from the library. I don't need anything else."

And I didn't. For two weeks I exercised on the floor. No mats. No videotapes. Nothing but me, a book of exercises from the library, and a determination that I had never felt before.

"I'm really proud of you," my husband finally admitted. "You didn't buy a thing this time. And you're sticking with it."

I beamed. "Right. But you know, this book talks about how those exercise bikes are one of the best workouts you can get. And you don't have to sit on the cold, hard floor."

Fear entered his eyes. "I spoke too soon."

"No. I just thought we might want to consider it for the future."

Two weeks later we had the bike. I had ridden it three times. It squeaked so loudly that our bird screamed nonstop when I rode it and the dog ran in frantic circles around it during my entire workout.

Today I bought that classified ad to sell the bike—or to trade it for an ice cream maker. And if I wait long enough and forget why I didn't ride it, I'll probably buy another one and go through the cycle again. Oops, pardon the pun.

✎ Put on the Cat's Oxygen Mask First

I had a very special "aha!" moment today.

It all started because I took a flight last year on one of those economy airlines. You know, the ones that have really good prices, but to compensate they ask the passengers to help with little things like cleaning the toilet and passing out pretzels. The ones that hire pilots so young that you know any moment they're going to come over the intercom saying, "Can somebody help me with this problem in my algebra homework?"

So, on that day, on that budget airline, I was actually listening to all the safety instructions very carefully. And that was when I heard it.

"In the event of an emergency, secure your oxygen mask first. Then take care of those around you who need assistance."

Whoa. That was it. That was the one piece of advice I should take in my life. I needed to take care of myself first. If not, then I wouldn't be of use to anyone else. It was a wonderful moment. I realized that I wasn't selfish if I helped myself; I was wise.

I decided to try it. I went home and signed up for a meditation class. When I got there, I found that the person who was in charge of the group was about to give up the practice sessions because of a lack of interest. So, what did I do?

I helped her create a newsletter and some advertising materials. I sent some e-mails to others I knew would be interested. I watched her business grow. And then I realized that I was out of the mood for meditation, so I moved on.

And since I still hadn't done anything for myself, I tried another adventure to give myself "oxygen." I decided to get back into writing. And since writers love company (so we can avoid actually having to write by talking about it), I joined a new writers' group. And ... well you know that process above with the newsletter, e-mails, and all that? Ditto. Time to move on and look for oxygen elsewhere.

I decided that I would become a hermit to help me take time out to use my oxygen mask. And, as a hermit, I started spending more time around the house. It was at this time I started really noticing the number of stray animals in my neighborhood. Thus, this relaxing time quickly became the period when I adopted Poe, Maddux, Sha Nay Nay, Rocky Raccoon, Elmo the Christmas Possum, and Gumbo and Etouffee, the twin squirrels.

Yes, my oxygen mask time now included such relaxing moments as cleaning litter boxes, breaking up disagreements between strays, and trying to avoid running over Elmo, who was now bold enough to stand behind my car when I had the nerve to try to leave the house without refreshing his food dish.

Today's "aha" moment was that I finally gave up. I realized it just wasn't going to happen. I reconciled myself to the fact that I was going to have to put the cat's oxygen mask on first. The possum's mask would be second. And mine would be somewhere between the raccoon and the squirrels. Sometimes it's just good to know where you come in the pyramid.

✎ *The Pig Chorus*

Today is my birthday, and every year on my birthday, I seem to end up reflecting on the world around me. For example, my favorite saying in life used to be: "Never try to teach a pig to sing. It wastes your time and annoys the pig."

Times have changed. I have matured. I have grown in understanding as well as waist size. I have listened to too many Tony Robbins, Stephen Covey, and Weird Al Yankovic tapes. So now my new favorite saying is: "They say, 'Never try to teach a pig to sing. It wastes your time and annoys the pig.' I say, 'Gimme a high C, Porky!'"

Thus, in the midst of my midlife crisis, I have discovered that the thrill of my existence is going against the grain that society offers us.

They ask whether the glass is half-full or half-empty. I say it doesn't matter—it just means it's time to call the waiter back.

They say, "Fake it till you make it." I say, "You'd better not stop then."

They say, "There are no problems, only opportunities." I say, "There are exceptions." My checking account is one that I might cite.

This is not to say that I'm a negative person. Quite the opposite. I have learned to be thrilled by the adventure of trying to balance my checkbook. I think of life as one giant amusement park ... and boy, am I amusing the bank.

I am now on my seventy-third career, my thirteenth cat, my fifth dog, my second bird, my first husband, and Prozac. I am often a downwardly mobile individual. I am not brilliant. I am not beautiful. I am not all that successful. However, I am housebroken, and I feel that this is a major accomplishment.

I am also a big enough person to admit that I am not brilliant, beautiful, or successful. On the other hand, if I weren't house-broken, I probably wouldn't mention that fact.

And so, in these, my midlife years, I have discovered that my experiences in life have helped me develop an appreciation of our "brothers of the swine" and a desire to train them to rise above their social standing, sing out loudly, and even perform show tunes (if they go in for that sort of thing).

Thus, for my birthday wish this year, I want to revel in the adventures of living in a world where pigs are learning to sing every day.

Saturday, September 1

✎ *Forty-Something and Slipping*

Today I'm forty-something plus one and all I can think about is how much like a roller coaster my life has been. I've been up on top of the hill. Then, with one sickening lurch of the stomach, I'm upside down, hanging on for dear life. I've been upside down for some time now. Luckily, I have a spouse who functions best upside down.

"You've got that depressed look again." He noted this as I toyed with the butter knife for much too long. "Are you out of Prozac again?"

"No, I'm just disappointed with life."

"Oh, we're disappointed again. What is it this time?"

"Well, it's my birthday week and what have I got to show for all my years?"

"Should I list alphabetically or chronologically this time?"

Understand that my husband was not being callous. It's just that we go through this discussion at least once a week, whether it's a birthday week or not.

"I know, I know. I've done a lot of wonderful things in the past. But what about now?"

"You're doing a lot of writing."

"No one is buying it."

"You've got me."

"You'll probably leave me for someone prettier."

"You know," he said, just a little worn out from this exchange, "I think we should try something different. How about if I point out the bad things and you defend yourself?"

I was dubious, but willing to try.

He started off. "You never clean the ceiling fans." He pointed up to the furry blades in our living room.

"Oh, now that's really low."

"No," he reminded me, "I'm playing bad cop. You tell me the good side."

"Well," I really had to think on this one, "When spring cleaning time comes, I'll really have a lot to keep me busy."

"Very good," he encouraged me. "What about that rejection letter you got this week from that editor?"

"I'll have the last laugh when she sees my book on the bestseller list."

"Great! What about the fact that everyone says your cooking is listed as a toxic substance in seven states?"

"Who says that?" I was immediately on the defensive.

"Well, you for one."

"Oh yeah."

"So, what do you say about that?"

"If God had wanted me to cook, he wouldn't have invented pizza delivery."

"You're doing really well. Now, what about the fact that you just had another birthday, you're not a size six, you're not rich and famous—"

I stopped him in mid-sentence, "Gee, you really know how to say those things that make a girl feel great."

"You've said those very same lines before. Answer them."

"Well," I tapped my chin. Somehow I always think better when I tap my chin. However, upon doing so, I discovered a pimple there.

"Good grief. I'm middle-aged. I have gray hairs. And I still have zits."

"That's not a good answer."

"Okay, okay. I guess the fact that I'm still at the bottom of my career means I have the chance to build and grow. And I can become rich and famous."

"Amen!" My husband was thrilled. "And what about that no-good husband of yours?"

Okay, one thing I don't handle well is when people fish for compliments. "When I'm successful, I'll ditch him and marry the hunk who played Hercules."

✎ Tennis … Courting Romance

If you're really bad at playing tennis, you know the signs that warn you to stay away from a court. If there are lots of people wearing white, stay clear. People who are good at tennis don't mind standing out. The rest of us try to blend into the background by wearing camouflage. Personally, I considered wearing outfits made of chain link so that I would really blend in.

Today my husband and I went out to play tennis for the first time in a long while. Or at least we called what we were doing playing tennis.

He hit the ball to me. I missed it. But in the process of missing it, I was somehow able to strike myself in the jaw with my own tennis racket. I spun around two or three times in slow motion and then dropped on my rear end in the middle of the court. At times like this I am glad that the aforementioned rear end has extra padding.

"Are you hurt?" He was concerned by the dazed expression on my face.

"William?"

"Who?"

"William Hurt. Are you asking me if I'm William Hurt?"

"No. I'm asking if you're injured."

"Oh yes, I'm insured."

"I think we might want to call it a day." He gently lifted me from the ground.

"Oh sure, you just want to quit because you got a point." I was not quitting while he was ahead.

"Okay then, that last point didn't count. We'll start over."

My husband is nothing if not a gentleman. I am nothing if not a poor sport.

"Are you about to slam?" I asked him.

"You mean serve?"

"Okay." I hit the ball over the net.

"Oh, *you're* serving now?"

"I just did," I pointed out to him.

"I see. Let's start over again."

"What's the score?" Scoring in tennis is something I have never gotten the hang of.

"Love."

"That's sweet, honey," I smiled.

"No, love means nothing."

I was crushed. "All the years I've given to you. The years when I could have been a famous model or actress. And it all meant nothing to you?"

"No, love is a way of scoring."

"Oh, so that's what it's all about with you boys. Only one thing on your mind. I should have known. I should have listened to the nuns at school."

"You're not grasping this. Love is how you score in tennis."

"Not in this game, it isn't. Boy, you think you know someone."

"You've been listening to *Who's on First?* again, haven't you?" Then he had me right where he wanted me. Confused. Of course, this is how I live most of my life. And he took the opportunity to serve a ball across the net. Amazingly, I missed it.

"Now I've got fifteen."

"See, that's all I wanted to know. All you had to do was to tell me the score."

"I've got fifteen," he repeated, "and you've got love."

"You're a hopeless romantic, you know that?" I smiled.

Wednesday, September 12

✎ Meditating Out Loud

The hardest thing in the world for me to do is to be silent. Yet I've tried to take it on as a hobby for the past few years. And to tell you the truth, I don't think it's working.

I have been trying meditation. You know, where you sit quietly and then wake up to find that you've been snoring instead of chanting a mantra. My episodes of meditation are often thwarted by a mind that refuses to sit still and insists on bringing up the most unmeditative-type thoughts. And, since it is truly biologically impossible for me to go any period of time without talking, I tend to meditate out loud.

Okay, I am now meditating. I am clearing my mind. I am not thinking of anything. Did I remember to deduct that debit from the checkbook when I bought toilet paper yesterday?

I am totally relaxed ... feeling great. And feeling like sitting on this hard floor is not very comfortable. *No, I'm feeling even more relaxed.* Relaxed, my foot. I know what's in store for me at work tomorrow. *Oh, so relaxed.* Except for the fact that I bet the house is on fire. And here I sit with my eyes closed, so I don't even know that the living room is now decorated in charcoal black. *So relaxed.* That would be really embarrassing if they came to put out the fire and found me stuck in this yoga position with my legs locked over each other.

I am at one with all of creation. Okay, maybe not all of creation—I'd really rather not be at one with Jerry Springer or Jeffrey Dahmer. Gee, what would I do if someone invited me to dinner and I found out that his last name was Dahmer?

I am in touch with a Higher Power. Higher than Tom Brokaw? How high up am I supposed to reach? There should be more guidelines for this stuff. I don't really think I'm getting anything out of this. Is this what Buddha did? I wonder if Buddha was really shaped like those hideous little statues of him. It just seems to me a great spiritual leader should have taken a little more pride in his appearance.

I'm listening to soothing music. Actually, I hate this music. Hearing the waves over the music makes it hard to tell if it's raining outside, which it probably is. I wonder if I put the car windows up. I wonder if I've meditated enough now. I'm getting pretty worn out from this relaxation stuff and I think my legs are permanently stuck in this position. This 'not thinking' thing is really tough.

And in the middle of all of this reverie, a voice comes to me, "Christee."

"Yeah?"

"I am a Higher Power."

"Seriously?"

"I wouldn't joke about a thing like this."

"Wow! And I suppose that you've come to me in this period of meditation to tell me something very important that will change my life."

"Yes."

"Oh, please tell me."

"First, yes, your car windows are up."

I was awestruck. A Higher Power had given me an all-important piece of knowledge. "And what else?" I asked.

"Nothing personal, but I'd prefer you not to meditate any more. You're wearing me out just listening."

Wisdom like that you can't get anywhere else but in meditation. It was truly amazing to me. It was even more amazing how much this Higher Power sounded like my husband trying to disguise his voice.

Either way, I decided it was a sign.

✑ Let There Be Light

I was just going to change a lightbulb. It was a simple enough task for a Thursday afternoon. But the best-laid plans of mice and men often breed leisure suits. And me trying to perform a simple act was not a best-laid plan.

It all started when I was too lazy to pull out the stepladder. The coffee table can hold the weight of my feet. Why not all of me? Maybe it's because it's a slatted table. Maybe it's because I haven't dieted enough in the last year. Or maybe it's because when I stood on the table and lifted my arms to the lightbulb fixture to make one turn of the screw, I was suddenly two feet shorter.

Yes, I fell through the table. And so, there I stood, too embarrassed to admit even to myself that I had destroyed a piece of my precious fiberboard furniture for a lightbulb. And there I stood until my husband got home—three hours later.

He surveyed the scene. "We had another domestic accident, did we?"

"A domestic accident is what my college buddy Carol had. They named her Tiffany. This is a domestic disaster."

"And what were we trying to do?"

"We were trying to change a lightbulb."

"Oh. No stepladder?"

"Too lazy."

"How long ago was this?"

"What day is this?"

"Uh huh. I see. And what are we going to do?"

"Never move again. It's too dangerous."

He had no comeback.

I pictured myself remaining there until my husband moved away to another city. The new owners would come in and find me in the living room, standing in the middle of the table. At first it would seem strange, but they would get used to me. At Christmas they might even hang a few ornaments on me. And no one would mind until I got older and started scaring the grandchildren.

"Grandma, the ugly old lady is staring at me."

And so, Grandma would finally decide it was time to redecorate. I would be placed out on the curb, waiting for the garbage truck. Someone would come along and see a perfectly good coffee table that could be repaired. But then they would spot the old lady in the middle of it.

"Naw, nothing's worth having something that ugly in the house." So, instead they would rummage through the garbage around me and pick up the black velvet painting of a matador to take home.

"I think I'm ready to move." I came back to the present and spoke to my husband.

He smiled knowingly and remarked, "Couldn't handle the idea of being rejected for a matador picture?"

"No. If it had been Elvis, it would have been different. But a nameless matador..." I cringed.

It wasn't until later that I realized I hadn't told him about the matador. Sometimes I think we're getting to be too much alike.

Sunday, September 23

✎ *Double Talk*

We say one thing and think something else. That makes for conversations something like the one I had with an old coworker this week. This person and I were barely acquaintances when we worked together. But for some reason, when two former coworkers run into each other in a new city, it creates a bond that is supposed to be sacred. And we knew that by this bond, we were expected to speak to one another. But we also both knew we had nothing in common.

I started the talk innocently enough. "Hi, how ya doin'?" Please, please, please, realize this is a rhetorical question. Don't go into detail.

There followed a fifteen-minute soliloquy about the problems of this man's life.

"What a shame." You don't really have a grasp of this socializing thing, do you?

I realized at this point, that this person was now firmly attached and not planning to end this conversation quickly. So I reached feebly for unimportant conversation filler.

"So, how's the cat?" The only member of his family that I had actually gotten along with.

"Dead."

"What a shame. How did he die?" Suicide, perhaps?

"Car."

"Oh." Don't tell me, he had a wreck in an escape attempt.

"Ran over him."

"Oh. And how's the wife?" Run over her, too?

"Still alive."

"Good." I'd hate to think of the damage those hips would do to a car bumper.

Now, I'd done my duty. Accordingly, I gave one of those gentle conversation enders.

"Beautiful day. Guess I'll head on out into it." Freedom, blessed freedom at last.

He didn't notice. "You know, this kind of sunshine can give you cancer."

"Is that so?" And did you know that this kind of conversation can give you the desire to meet more mimes?

"Yup."

And then, I did the ultimate conversation ender. I stopped talking. But, for some people, this is too subtle. And so, we both stood, staring in opposite directions past each other. Then I glanced at my watch. This was even less subtle, but still not blatant enough, for he spoke again.

"Meeting to go to?"

I answered, "Appointment." Uh oh. This conversation had just reached that dangerous point. Yes, it was now a conversation without verbs. This is not to be confused with a nonverbal conversation, which would probably have been more interesting at this point. No, now I had resorted to sentence fragments to get the idea across that I was in a hurry to leave.

"Where?"

"Downtown." Far downtown. Far, far away from here. Please let me be free. Let my people go.

"Where downtown?"

"Fifth Street." Now can I go? Or do I have to promise an organ before you'll let me escape? "Well, I guess I'd better get going. Can't afford to be late."

"I'm headed downtown, too. I guess I'll see if I can catch a cab."

"Oh." No, I won't ask. I refuse to ask. You can't make me.

And there was a pregnant pause. I tried not to speak. But suddenly my tongue took on a mind of its own and said aloud, "Need a ride?"

"Sure."

"Great, and maybe we can catch up on the rest of your family on the ride." !@#$%*!!

✎ Give Me Liberty or Give Me Cash. In Fact, Forget the Liberty, I'll Take Tens and Twenties.

I am obsessed by the idea of money. But then, what do we expect? We live in a world where all that is talked about is how to make it, how to invest it, how to save it, how to make more of it, how to make it grow, how to use it, how to charge instead of using it, how to give it, how to hide it, how to spend it, and how to look like you have more of it than you do. If I weren't obsessed, I'd be worried.

However today this obsession took me to a psychiatrist, which costs about seventy-five dollars an hour of that money.

After perching on the edge of her requisite psychiatrist's couch, I began. "I think about money constantly. I always worry about having enough of it."

"Do you have enough of it?"

"No."

"Why do you feel that way?"

"Because I can't afford this visit."

I thought she was going to throw me out, but she found out I had insurance.

"So, you don't have enough money for the things you need?"

"No. But I do have bill collectors who send me congratulations cards when I take on extra part-time jobs."

"Do you spend more than you should?"

"Well, the TV always tells me to."

"You mean the commercials?"

"No, the TV. When it's off, some voice comes out of it and tells me to buy things."

"So, you're hearing voices?"

"Oh yeah, I'd forgotten about that."

"And you feel obsessed."

"Yes. With everything I do, I think about how I could make money doing it. My hobbies, my talents, sex. I get upset when I do any of these things for free."

"How does your husband feel about this?"

"He's thinking about taking out a loan."

"Oh."

"I can't do anything for fun. I can't read a book unless it's a self-help book. I can't take a class without trying to figure out how to do something with it to make money to pay for the class. I can't go anywhere without thinking about how I can get rich. I want to make lots of money. I want to go into Burger King and say 'One of each.' I want to buy a car that costs more than my house."

"So you have trouble relaxing?"

"Yes. I can never do one thing at a time. I always sit in front of the television with something to work on in my lap. I can't go walking because there's no possibility of money in it, unless I find a quarter on the street. Last month I finally made myself find the time to grow a garden. Then I sold all my vegetables."

"Yes. I can see how you have a problem. How do you feel about this?"

"I'm upset. I want to learn to live on the money I have, not money I don't have. I want to cut up my credit cards. I want to stop being a money addict."

"That's how you see yourself?"

"Yes. A money addict. I can never have enough."

"I see." She was writing all this down.

"So, Doc, what can I do? What could help me? Is there any hope for me at all?"

"I'd love to talk with you about it some more, but we're out of time."

I walked out, realizing that this woman had done nothing for sixty minutes but sit and listen to me talk and ask a few questions. And she had made seventy-five dollars. I drove straight to the local college and signed up for the next psychology course.

✎ Falling for Fun and Sympathy

Everyone has done it at one time or another. Tripped over something that wasn't there. And we always look back and glare at the offending item—or at least the place where the offending item would be if it really existed. But this morning, I tripped on air. There wasn't even anything near enough to blame it on. And I was not amused.

I had just stepped out of a van, closed the door, and turned to walk away with an armful of items, when suddenly one of those involuntary jerks took over my body. Usually, I only get those strange muscle jerks when I am dozing off at night. But this one visited during the daylight hours.

One moment, I was a basically normal human being. The next moment I was a flailing, wailing mass of humanity. The bags I was carrying flew in three different directions. My body fell northward. My foot faced eastward. And the parking lot under my leg ... well, I guess you could say it moved painward.

And so, there I was, sprawled in a parking lot on a major street. And of course, cars passing by felt obligated to honk and laugh, thinking that I had performed this swan dive for their entertainment.

From the distance, I heard a security guard yelling, "Do you need an ambulance?" As I slipped from consciousness, I was able to summon the breath to yell back, "I've fallen and I can't get up." A comedienne to the end. And worse yet, a comedienne with outdated material.

I'm not sure why I am as clumsy as I seem to be. I have fallen over everything known to man—animal, mineral, and pillow. I have cut myself on items ranging from knives to peach pits to toilet paper dispensers. I have hit my head on cabinets when less than three minutes prior someone has said, "Look out for that cabinet door." And my personal physician, otherwise known as my husband, deals with each of these crises and will inevitably handle this morning's parking lot incident the same way.

"Poor thing," he always says in his best "I'll make it better" voice. "Here, let me fix you some Epsom salts to soak in."

At this point in our ritual, I'm not really that badly hurt, but the idea of being waited on appeals to me, so I acquiesce. And it's amazing that, with each act of kindness he performs, I feel worse.

Yes, the sore ankle begins to manifest itself in the form of a headache. And, of course, the sore back from that fall begins to bother me.

Pillows are brought. Aspirins are delivered. Meals begin to miraculously appear. Now, I know I shouldn't enjoy an injury, but at this point, it's pretty hard to rationalize that I'm well enough to go on with life as usual. So my sore ankle and I sit back, watch reruns of *The Brady Bunch*, and are waited on until guilt gets the better of us. Then it's back to life as usual.

The funny thing is that, in this cycle, the real pain seems to appear two days later. And by then I've used up all my invalid status. So, at the time when it really starts to hurt, I can't take advantage of it.

But it's okay. I know I'll have yet another invalid vacation because, with my lifestyle, another injury is never far away. Perhaps it's because I never listened to my mother when she gave me all those wonderful warnings in my childhood. She warned me that my face would stick like that. She tried to tell me that sticks and stones could be hazardous to my health, but words couldn't hurt me. Little did we know that, in reality, tripping over sticks, stones, and words would be my biggest problems in life.

I did listen to one piece of advice she gave me. When I was very small, she warned me not to touch the stove because it was hot. I've been careful not to touch one since then. I let the pizza delivery people take that chance instead.

✎ The Joys of Parenthood, or "Please Hit Me With That Skillet"

On the upcoming occasion of my parents' anniversary, I find myself getting a little sentimental, a little reflective, and a little older. And I'm about to write them for money again. It makes me think of the injustices we heaped upon these unsuspecting people known as parents and makes me marvel at those who take on the job of parenthood. A twenty-four-hour-a-day job with no retirement benefits and bosses who are shorter than you. A job that gives you gray hair, ulcers, and occasionally, a warm feeling.

I remember the way my mother found herself frequently looking in the mirror for age lines after one of her kids asked her if she had voted for Lincoln. She had the task of masking outrage when the kids at school showed me that weaving a pencil through my fingers made one stand up in a way that infuriated the teacher. "Why should my finger make her mad, Mommy? She never minds when I put up my whole hand."

And, of course, the bathroom wall had a whole new vocabulary for Mommy to explain away to her little darlings.

"That word dear, is like when kitty goes to the litter box. No, that's not exactly how Mr. Brown meant it when he stubbed his toe in his front yard." From her I learned that, if you smile when you do it, even an ear washing seems like an act of God.

And she did the impossible as well as the improbable. She made a Halloween costume out of her cocktail dress. She always lost her appetite when there was just one helping of ice cream left.

And even when she was crying through the last few minutes of *Camelot* on television, she let her kids change the channel to a terrible sitcom. She let us learn to drive in her new Impala. She acted thrilled every Mother's Day when we gave her the same two-dollar dusting powder. And she smiled brilliantly through all of our weddings, although we suspected she cried those nights.

Time went on and "mom" became synonymous with "Thank God she's here."

Dad didn't get to be around as much when his kids were growing up. For the most part he was in some other place doing the things he did best—working and worrying.

His child was born and he was there, beaming happiness from ear to ear. He held this little bundle and marveled at its size, its little fingers and ears, its sounds, and the fact that it was seeping through onto his shirt. Into every life some rain must fall.

He worked all day and wondered if this little person would remember him when he got home. He arrived home and received the little bundle for his allotted time. More rain. It never failed.

Since he missed out on the everyday specialties that Mother instilled, he worried because he wasn't around when the bundle learned to think on its own. "How can she be the lead in the senior play? She just learned to say 'daddy' three weeks ago."

And though he was sometimes played off as the bad guy ("Just wait till your father gets home"), it's amazing how, when family finances were at their worst, he managed to produce that Baby First Step I drooled over. And when I permed my hair and looked like an overused Q-tip, he pointed out that I always was a trendsetter. And how, when he claimed to hate that darned cat, he's the one who built an elaborate coffin when it died, and I could swear I saw moisture in his left eye.

Here's to the man who taught me the meaning of the phrase "gentle giant" and to the woman whose patience never ran thin.

✎ Radio: The Great Preoccupation

Yes, right now I'm self-employed, also known as "occupationally challenged." I've had lots of jobs—lots and lots of jobs, in fact. Whenever I get really passionate about my job, I throw myself into it so much that I lose all balance in my life. Where is that happy medium? Obviously running a séance in some other part of the country.

Today, as I sat listening to the latest music by groups whose names sound like health problems, I thought back to my first job.

Radio. Oh yes, I loved working in radio. But a job where you have a phone line to allow small children and social outcasts to constantly rate your performance is worse than any evaluation from a nasty boss.

Some of the stations where I worked—well, I should have had a clue they weren't going to stay in business from the start. For instance, at one station where I worked I got locked out of the control room on a Sunday for over an hour. Nobody noticed. Nobody even called. We were off the air all this time and not even the boss was listening. I should have guessed our ratings were low when I noticed that our sign was made of rub-on vinyl letters.

Radio people are a different breed. I remember one fellow who was so ugly that the station refused to put his picture on the wall with the rest of the disc jockeys. He moved away one night. In the middle of the night, he just packed up all his furniture in his pickup truck and headed off into the darkness.

That wouldn't have been such a problem, except that he had been renting a furnished apartment.

Then I worked with a real creep whose failed hair transplant made him look like a character from an alien movie. He called the listeners filthy names on the air. Last I heard he was still in radio. He was also in court.

One guy I worked with locked himself in the control room and played a single song over and over until the police broke in and took him away. You might expect the song to be something meaningful like "Take This Job and Shove It" or "We Are The World." But no, he played "Old Rivers" by Walter Brennan for three straight hours. Poor fellow. He made his big social statement and nobody could understand it.

Back when drugs were common in radio, you often had the problem of the jock after you coming in wearing his underwear on top of his head to keep the government from reading his thoughts. One night my replacement came in at midnight screaming that his skin was on fire. Obviously he was on really expensive drugs. His usual ones just had him screaming that his skin was hot. Now, I'm compassionate and understanding and all that stuff, but when it comes time to get off the air and go home, all that empathy goes out the window. I threw water on him to put out the fire and sat him down at the control board to work.

I tried to run away from the grown-up business world about two years ago. I returned to the great world of radio to try to recapture my glory days. Let me tell you that in these later years, I don't think we have the patience that is required for radio. I proved it when someone called in, saying he was angry that I didn't play his song and then he threatened me with the age-old line, "I know the owner."

I answered him with a new age line, "Me too. Real geek, isn't he?" It was a simple moment, but it reminded me that there is a time to get out of the sandbox and let the younger kids play. I left radio for good.

✎ Hiding Away the Manilow

As the years go by and I become more pseudo-intellectual, I discover more and more things that I enjoy, but refuse to admit that I enjoy. This fact hit me as I walked by my album collection—yes, I still own records—and noted that I had put all my classical collections in the front. But underneath those was the unthinkable. I could never let anyone see that, once you got past the classics, the rock, and the new age, hidden deep in my collection was the complete set of Barry Manilow albums. And worse yet, I listen to them sometimes. And sometimes I get caught.

"I'm home." My husband walked in from a day at the coalmines. Strange, since he works at an architectural firm.

"How was your day?" It was the wifely thing to ask.

"Fine. What have you been doing?" he asked innocently.

"Nothing."

"Oh, surely you've been doing something."

"Well, listening to some music," I muttered, rearranging the nearly dead flowers on the table for the twelfth time.

He studied me closely. "You've been listening to him again, haven't you?"

I mumbled something and kicked at a dust bunny.

"I worry about you."

"I still like Barry Manilow."

"That's fine. But why can't you admit it?"

"It's just not done."

"You worry too much about what other people think."

"Wrong." I disagreed, kicking the dust bunny under the couch.

"Let's recap, shall we?" My husband is particularly good at recapping when it's stuff about me that he's listing. "For years we had to tell people you had a rare disease that only flared up on Saturday nights because you didn't want to admit that you were a *Love Boat* fan."

"Well, I wouldn't call me a fan ..."

"Next, you watched *Highway to Heaven* for years on a miniature television in the bathroom."

"Shhhhh. Someone might hear you."

"And what about the fact that you love to read romance books, but you have to hide them inside the cover of the latest John Irving novel?"

"Doesn't everybody?"

"There are so many things you love and won't admit that you love."

"Name three."

"The smell of mimeographed sheets of paper from our school days, the television series *Hercules*, and that feeling after a really good sneeze."

"Well ..." I couldn't disagree.

"And you pretend to like things like opera, those 'critically acclaimed movies' that don't make sense, and aerobics classes."

"You'd never tell anyone this, would you?" I feared for my life.

"Will you try to stop worrying about what other people think?"

"You mean, free myself from my adult ideas of what I'm supposed to like and dislike? You mean, admit things like the fact that I don't watch the president's speeches? I just wait for Tom Brokaw to tell me what he said. Admit that I read the classifieds every weekend and imagine myself in other jobs?"

"Right! That's the spirit. Admit that you actually like computers. Admit that you dreamed of being on the comedy competition on *Star Search*. Admit that you're afraid to go to the dentist and haven't been to one since the time you cracked a tooth while disco dancing."

"You mean, throw off the shackles of what other people think and live my own life?"

"Right! Be yourself. Be proud of your feelings."

"I can do it," I shouted. "I'm free! I can even tell the world that I love Partridge Family music."

My husband looked astonished. "Well, let's not get carried away."

✎ Holiday Mania

I am a total and absolute geek when it comes to holidays. I love them. I can't help myself. I am totally enamored of all the materialistic things that come with holidays.

So, while people complain about the commercialization of all our major holidays, I'm calling a home shopping channel to ask, "How much is that Santa bourbon decanter with the screw-off head and simulated ruby nose?"

And so, last week, I found myself fighting a dozen children at a discount store to get at the dancing, screaming skeleton with flashing eyes. He doesn't really scream. It's more of a warble. He doesn't really dance, either. He just hangs there and gyrates a little obscenely. But his eyes do flash. Sure, it was a terrible waste of money. Sure, it's something a child should buy, not a quasi-adult. Sure, next week I plan to go buy the matching dancing, screaming pumpkin with flashing teeth—on sale.

I love Halloween. I believe that people's costumes often hide deeply repressed fantasies. Some aren't so well hidden. Every year we see French maids, harem dancers, hookers, and Tarzans with overlapping stomachs lurking at Halloween parties. They seem to be in search of French homeowners, Arab sheiks, pimps, and a few good monkeys. But my costumes have included everything from a California Medfly to a land mine, when I wore a pie plate on top of my head. I worry about what hidden fantasies these costumes reveal about me.

Then Thanksgiving rolls around. A holiday with no true purpose besides eating ourselves into a turkey coma, wondering how they'll change Bart Simpson's balloon into a more recent cartoon character, and shopping for the next holiday.

This is a good holiday. I never appreciated Thanksgiving when I was younger. It was always just something to get past to reach Christmas. But I did get out of school for it, so it had some merit. And I usually got to dress up like a Pilgrim or a turkey, and that was fun, since I was already depressed about having to wait another year for a Halloween costume.

But now I appreciate Thanksgiving for the fact that I don't have to buy gifts for anyone. A holiday where MasterCard and Visa are not the big winners is a good holiday for me. But creating uses for leftover turkey gets a little trying. Hint: Turkey is not good with pineapple.

Then comes the biggie. We wait all year for Christmas. It lasts twelve minutes to those of us with the childlike mentality that believes the true excitement of the holiday is found only in those moments when we are surrounded by wrapped gifts and pine needles.

After those twelve minutes, depression sets in. I suddenly realize I waited a month for each of those minutes, and those twelve months will pass again before I can open those wrappings and once again discover that my niece has given me an eraser shaped like a Powerpuff Girl.

New Year's Day is anticlimactic. Sure, it's a new beginning. Sure, it's a time for resolutions. And sure, it's the day of the year the Alka Seltzer people live for and the only time people actually eat black-eyed peas. But it just can't compete with a Christmas tree that rotates and plays, "I Saw Mommy Kissing Santa Claus." Perhaps if we came up with a few New Year's songs that people can understand the words to (What is an auld lang syne, anyway?), a couple of good things to eat on New Year's Day (trading the black-eyed peas for something coated in chocolate or confectioners sugar), and a few New Year's games (like *Pin the Diaper on the New Year's Baby*), we could save this holiday from being forgotten in the haze of hangovers and ignored resolutions. Or, we could just start our Valentine's Day shopping earlier.

✎ This Meeting is Now Called to Disorder

Clubs are scary. They can take over your life and you never even realize they've done it. I've lived through quite a few of them, but it took sheer determination to escape. It's what I imagine a cult to be like. You try to get away, but then someone calls you to work on just one bake sale and the next thing you know you're organizing a march on the state capital to raise money for homeless sea turtles. I never even meant to join my neighborhood watch group—I went to talk to the director once, and boom, I ended up not only joining, but I quickly became the leader of this committee. Running the meetings for these groups is always an experience. This evening's neighborhood watch group meeting was no exception.

"This meeting is now called to order." I knew the group wasn't ready to get down to business, but I had to break them out of their reverie. It's that perverse side of me that wants to see what's going to happen at this one. It's the same side of me that imagines it will get important news from a show called *Judge Judy*.

"Should it be called to order yet? Jane's not here." The gray-haired secretary noted this.

"Jane's going to be late," the treasurer responded.

"Perhaps we should wait to start the meeting?" The secretary was worried.

"Jane said to start without her," the treasurer informed the group.

Someone else decided to join in this inauspicious beginning to a meeting. "Jane's the one who always says the pledge."

"Well," I suggested, "someone else can say the pledge today."

I saw embarrassed glances around the table. "Someone else does know the pledge, don't they?"

Glances again.

"We'll dispense with the pledge. Old business?"

"I don't think we have any," the secretary admitted.

"Great." I hate going over old stuff anyway. "New business?"

"I don't think we have any of that either." The secretary again.

"Well, that's interesting. Why are we here?"

"We have to have a meeting every month." This came from a tiny girl who appeared to be hiding behind a huge notebook.

"Why?"

"To plan new business."

"Okay. Let's plan." I was trying to get something useful from this meeting, and I was really starting to see why, at my second meeting, they had elected me president when I went to the bathroom. "So, what can we do?"

Silence.

"Garage sale?" I finally suggested.

The treasurer piped up. "We had one last year."

"Okay." I was not going to ask why we couldn't have one again. "How about a training seminar?"

"We've never done that before."

"Good." I was pleased.

"There must be a reason we haven't done one before," someone else added.

"True." The little old lady at the end of the table looked up from her knitting. "I don't know what the reason is, but it must be good or we'd have done a seminar before."

"Yes," the woman at my side who was taking up two chairs agreed. "I vote against a seminar." Murmurs of agreement ensued.

"All right," I demurred. "Let's hear some other ideas."

"A garage sale?" The girl at the other side of the table woke up.

"Great idea," the little old lady threw in. "We haven't done one of those since last year."

"Yeah," a general voice of agreement arose from the group.

"Hey, look," the secretary shouted, "Jane's here!"

For the next fifteen minutes the group was saying hello to Jane. Then the secretary looked at me. "I guess we can call the meeting to order now."

Swaying to the Music In My Chair

I received an invitation today to my twenty-fifth high school reunion. Why would I want to go to a high school reunion? These people know me from the worst years of my life. My formative years. Those years when I humiliated myself daily. To go back to visit would simply throw me back into the role I played during those days—court jester. And holding my breath for two or three days to appear to have a waistline is not an enticing proposition either. We all try to correct the image that we created in high school in these two-day gatherings. Not possible.

But the invitation does bring back some interesting memories.

I remember my first high school dance. What a trauma. I wore a bra that had a personality of its own—and two feet of padding. It was strapless, too. I remember putting my arms around my date's neck for the first dance and feeling the strapless bra slip down around my waist. I was so sure *The Enquirer* would pop out of nowhere for a picture of the girl with two sets of breasts.

He had never been on a date either. I think he was twenty-seven. He was a geek. Bless his heart, he was a sweet geek, but a geek by any other name … well, you know. He was a blind date. I would have preferred a seeing-eye dog's company.

The fun part was before the dance. Every female in the family felt like it was her duty to show me how to dance. The only problem with this comes when one realizes that dance steps changed yearly during my youth. My mother demonstrated the box waltz. I was certain I had not seen this one on *American Bandstand.* But I tried. Mother's ingrown toenail never had such a workout.

Then it was my oldest sister's turn. She showed me how to put one hand on my partner's shoulder, hold his other hand, and dance gently around the room. I felt like Ginger Rogers. Unfortunately, Ginger Rogers was in black and white movies, so I thought maybe this style was outdated, too.

My other sister showed me how people put both arms around the neck and dance closely in a small circle. It was an intimate dance, and one that seemed appropriate based on what I had seen on television lately. Mother decided we would go back to the box waltz.

I never did learn to dance that night. It was all right though. My little geek didn't know how to dance either. He took pictures the whole night. He was so thrilled that he had finally made it to a dance. I was so thrilled when I finally made it home. We didn't kiss goodnight. He shook my hand, took a last picture of my corsage, and left. I should have married him.

Wednesday, November 14

✎ Mom is a Four-Letter Word

My mother just doesn't understand me. She threatens me frequently with retroactive abortion. I threaten her with Pleasant Manor. I tell her if she's going to leave me her twenty-seven-inch color television when she kicks off, why not give it to me now while the darn thing still works right?

Actually, I wouldn't change a hair on her lip. Although I did once spend seventy-five dollars an hour to have a therapist tell me that I had a conflict with my mother. Big surprise. I could have spent just twenty-five dollars more and had Guido who lives on the corner take care of that conflict for good.

Today my mom and I tried to go shopping together. It was not pretty.

"Christee, this would look great on you." She held up an outfit that looked like something you would buy for a doll.

"It's a Barbie Doll outfit. It's just not me, Mom."

"But it's pretty."

"That's why it's not me. I'm not the *pretty* type. I like functional clothes."

"This is functional. It has pockets."

"It also has lace around the collar."

"What's wrong with that?"

"I'm already married. I don't need to wear lace more than once in my lifetime."

She gave up and started to move on. A saleslady approached us. "Can I help you?"

I could have told her that was a mistake. Mom dove right in. "Well, that's a lovely outfit you have on."

"Thank you." She didn't realize she was being set up. I did.

"Is that lace on the sleeves?" Oh, this was about to get good.

"Well, yes it is." Like a lamb to the slaughter.

"Oh, is your name Barbie?"

"Ma'am?"

"Are you getting married today?"

This woman was looking really nervous. She looked to me for help. I was not helping. She got herself into this; she could get herself out of it.

Mom continued, "Is it possible that lace is not just for wedding days and dolls?"

"Certainly." She was trying to humor this woman. I could have told her that was a mistake. I'd been trying to do it for over forty years and it had never worked for me.

"So my daughter could wear lace if she wanted to?"

"Certainly." It had seemed a safe word once, so she tried it again.

"So, she must not want to."

The saleslady looked at me in my faded jean overalls meant for a man twice my size. "I don't think she wants to."

"Aha!" Mom smiled. She had won. She had gotten someone to admit that I just don't like lace. She walked off victoriously toward the bathing suits, ready to find one with a built-in bra that was three sizes too large so that it would make my waist look thinner.

The saleslady looked at me.

I shrugged. "We're out of her medicine."

"Is she dangerous?"

"Only if you have her genes."

Wednesday, November 21

✎ Culinary: English for "Don't Try This at Home"

I sometimes wonder why nobody comes to my house for dinner. But then, I realize that, if the state of my house—which includes a dog who has had many years of urinary tract problems and a cat whom the pet psychic would probably say uses hairballs to get attention—wasn't overwhelming to potential visitors, then my lack of culinary ability would probably keep them away.

And this week, when the family has everyone bring one dish for the Thanksgiving dinner, don't think I haven't noticed that they asked me to bring the bags of ice.

It's hard for me to concentrate on cooking. It's so impermanent. I want to do things that will last forever. Cooking only lasts until the next meal, or until the salmonella wears off. But I have tried lately. Here is one of my favorite recipes:

Jambalaya Recipe

✓ First you look for the leftovers in your refrigerator that have no green spots (unless you've actually remembered to purchase something from the vegetable kingdom).

✓ Then you find the leftovers that have no "fur" growing on them.

✓ Now you have the ingredients that are necessary for my recipe—jambalaya. *Jambalaya* is a Louisiana word that means, "anything from your Frigidaire that is not green or furry … with rice."

✓ The first thing to do with jambalaya is to cook the meats in lard. This ensures that any healthy aspect that might have been hiding in there is gone.

✓ Now, put in rice and then add enough seasonings to make even someone named "T-Boy" cry.

✓ Then burn it. Serve with enough beer so that no one notices that the dish is burned. Simple, isn't it?

Other recipes that I have tried lately are:

✓ Fondue: My husband insists "fondue" is French for "Cook it your own damn self."

✓ Mediterranean foods such as kibbi and grape leaves: These are family dishes that I am trying to learn to cook. However, I'm having a hard time getting past the traditions that go into the cooking of these dishes. For example, between each step of preparing the meat for kibbi, a shot of bourbon is required. No one in the family actually remembers anything that comes after the second step of making this dish.

✓ Turbo-Cooker meals: A Turbo-Cooker is a really cool pot that lets you burn meals in a fraction of the time. It reduces cooking time and lets you concentrate on fun things like seeing how well your smoke detector works and how long it takes for the pizza delivery guy to get there.

✓ Crock Pot meals: A crock pot is a really cool pot that lets you burn meals in a lot longer time. These let you cook all day and then concentrate on fun things like trying to clean the stuff out of the pot and working on that pizza delivery thing again.

My next culinary lesson is how to make attractive place cards that include the emergency room phone number.

Saturday, November 24

✎ Quest for Fun

I recently realized that in my fast-paced, "see how quickly this latest get-rich-quick scheme can fail" lifestyle, I had totally forgotten how to have fun. The realization hit me when I noticed that my idea of excitement was watching the clock on the bank sign change minutes.

Another indication came from the fact that colored chalk could have such a different effect on me than it did in those wonderful days of my youth.

I remember as a child, drawing hopscotch squares, sketching pictures that almost resembled flowers and trees, and writing haiku on the sidewalks. But this week, I was on the patio at a restaurant where they brought out colored chalk to amuse the children. Naturally, I needed to be amused more than they did, so I took it from the youngsters at the adjoining table. Then I sat to decide what to draw.

A moment grew into quite a few moments. And it wasn't until dessert that I finally drew my masterpiece on the concrete patio. It was a chalk body outline. I think I may have missed the point.

I don't get it. I used to have fun with something as simple as yelling, "Red Rover, Red Rover, send Stumpy right over." Now I only enjoy yelling that during debates at Board of Directors' meetings.

I just don't know how to have fun anymore. I discussed this with my low-cost analyst, also known as my husband.

"David, I want to do something fun."

"That's nice."

"No, it's not. I don't know what's fun anymore."

I saw that trapped look in his eyes—like a deer in headlights, like a cat held too tightly by a three-year-old, and like my mother when we ask her who gets the good china in her will. He knew this meant that I was about to launch into a major discussion. He wanted to run. But he stayed to talk because he is strong. Because he is understanding. And because I was holding his car keys.

"Okay," he began, "what do you like to do?"

"Sleep."

"That's a start."

"I don't think it's considered one of the main hobbies, arts, or crafts."

"Well, what other things do you like to do?"

"Buy things."

"The thank-you cards from Visa have shown us that."

"Yeah, but the certified letter to 'cease and desist' from Visa also makes that impossible anymore."

"What else?"

"I don't like to do anything else."

"The only things you like in life are sleeping and shopping?" He was incredulous.

"Well, sometimes I like to combine the two. That home shopping channel is pretty fun late at night."

"It's also how we ended up with the Santa decanter with the screw-off head."

"That could double, perhaps even triple, in value in our lifetime," I quoted dutifully from the blurb on the side of the box.

"What about your self-help tapes? You really used to enjoy that sort of thing."

I thought about it. He was right. I love self-help tapes, books, or anything like that. I have meditated myself through a few of my more traumatic birthdays. I have listened to subliminal meditation tapes that have ocean waves and music and, I believe, a quiet voice that tells me to "buy more tapes." I have read books on every career, hobby, and psychological disorder known to man. I even read a book called *How to Disappear*

Without a Trace. Amazingly enough, they let me pay for that with a check.

Yes, he was right. I like self-help and do-it-yourself materials. So I went right out and bought a kit on a brand new subject. Though it took awhile, I managed to find a subject that I hadn't studied before.

And, since this was his idea, I don't understand why he wasn't pleased when I came home with my *Do-It-Yourself Divorce Kit.*

✎ *Public-Relations Challenged*

I think I made a mistake today. I asked my husband to be my Public Relations Manager for my writing. It reminded me that he is a wonderful man, but far from normal.

One of his suggested slogans for promotion of my book was, "Shut up and buy the book." His other slogans included:

✓ Buy the book—you don't want us to have killed these trees in vain.

✓ Buy the book ... because other sleep aids can be addictive.

✓ She's not Hemingway, but she's sober.

✓ It's real ink. Taste it!

✓ Don't wait for the movie. There won't be one. Buy the book now.

✓ A great gift for Arbor Day.

✓ The Quicker Picker Upper. (I had to explain to him that this one was already taken and that I would prefer not to sell the book as an absorbent paper product.)

He wants to do television interviews for me, but he insists on using his alter ego, Guapo the Sock Puppet, who affects a rather pronounced accent and tends to use expletives and abusive language on a regular basis.

David also wrote a letter regarding my public appearances, in which he outlines rules such as these:

- ✓ Never, under any circumstances, allow anyone on your staff to look directly at Ms. Atwood or her image as represented by a reflection.

- ✓ Remove all Harry Potter and Bobby Knight products and collateral marketing/merchandise at least forty-eight hours prior to Ms. Atwood's arrival.

- ✓ Supply 3-D glasses for all attendees with "red lens" and "blue lens" reversed. It is not required to reverse the lenses of the 3-D glasses that will be on the life-sized inflatable "Kevin Sorbo as Hercules" mannequin that will arrive via courier the morning of the event.

- ✓ Ms. Atwood reserves the right to address each employee and/or attendee by the name "Mojo."

Yes, my husband is not normal. But his heart is in the right place. He wants my writing career to be successful. He believes in my writing ability. And he wants his next birthday gift to be more chrome for his motorcycle.

And so, I don't know that I can fire him from his position as my Public Relations Manager. Perhaps I'll just promote him to an executive position. I believe that's the level where people actually stop working. And that's exactly how he would be most helpful to me.

✎ Kmart's on Fire and I'm in the Express Lane

I went to Kmart this weekend. I was buying one item, but I was in line behind three other people buying many, many items—without price tags—and apparently paying for them in pennies. When I finally got to the front of the line, I heard screaming and watched as a female employee ran to the counter yelling, "I'll call the fire department."

Yes, there was a fire in the infant department. And I did what any good shopper would do in this predicament. I turned to the young cashier who was ready to race to the nearest exit and ordered, "You have time. Check me out."

Priorities. You've got to set them.

Every so often I re-evaluate my priorities. It's usually pretty depressing. When I returned home after my trip to Kmart, I discussed these priorities with David.

"So, I want to be a writer. That's my main purpose in life and the reason I left my old job."

A grunt of agreement from my husband.

"Well, actually I guess being rich is even more of a priority than that."

Grunt, grunt.

"Retiring early. I forgot that one."

Even the grunts stopped.

"I want to act, too."

This raised an eyebrow.

"I want to be an entertainer. One of those all-around entertainers. Yeah, and maybe I'll learn to sing."

"May I say something?" Usually my husband is not so bold. I was shocked into silence, but only for a moment.

"Did you think of another priority I forgot?"

"I just think maybe you ought to set more realistic priorities for yourself. You're setting yourself up for failure. And with failure comes depression. And with depression I have to listen to those long speeches about how fat you feel, how you hate your nose, and why I don't make more money."

I thought this over. Maybe he's right. Maybe I should be more realistic. Maybe I should appreciate the goals I've already reached. But it seems that every time I reach a goal, I forget that it was a goal.

You know, it's like when you're a kid, and all you dream of is graduating from high school. Then you finally graduate and you find yourself shrugging, "Well, that was no big deal. But it will really be something when I graduate from college." Then you graduate from college. And then it's, "Yeah, but it's just a stupid bachelor's degree. No big deal."

Then you reach other goals. "When I'm thirty, I'll be totally grown up." Then you hit thirty and realize that you still do dashboard drumming along with songs on the car radio, you're still bored by people on television who analyze the national budget, and you still find yourself with hangovers after parties.

So you feel you've ruined yet another milestone.

I thought about how happy we could be if we savored the stage we're at, instead of searching for new challenges before the old achievements have even lost their shine. If only we could say, "I really accomplished something today." If we didn't always qualify what we had done with, "Yeah, but it would have been better if..."

And so, I agree with my husband. I'll set more realistic priorities. Sure I'm still keeping my goals of being a writer, rich, retired, and entertaining people, but I'll give up on that singing thing. I feel much better now that I'm being so practical.

Wednesday, December 12

✎ David's Shining Moment ... and Scalp

I came home late last night to find my husband wearing a towel over his head. This did not bode well.

"I'm guessing that this is not a tribute to my Lebanese heritage."

"Voila!" He pulled off the towel. There was a freshly shaved head underneath.

Mind you, this was not a total shock. I have been prepared for this by the fact that his bald spot was trying to meet his receding hairline and we had already had the talk about how he would never take those last three strands and try to stretch them across his head.

But, on the other hand, I had become strangely attached to those last few forehead hairs. So attached, in fact, that we had named them.

"So Allen is gone?"

"With Larry and Elmo," he nodded. "But I'm not sure if this is permanent. I just wanted to try it out. What do you think?" It actually looked okay. It was just a shock to see the gleam of the untanned scalp reflecting in the lamplight.

"I think it looks okay. But it needs a tan."

No great lesson here. Just a realization that hair, along with most other things, is more expendable than we realize.

My husband disappeared into the bathroom to admire the shine on his head. When he emerged, he had yet another piece of wisdom for this special night.

"Here's something to remember," he noted as he saw that I was writing in my journal. "It's difficult, but not impossible, to kill a mosquito with a toilet brush."

A bald head and wisdom like that. It's like having my own little Buddha.

✎ God, Joyce Kilmer, and Dad

Christmastime brings back interesting memories. Our family had such unique traditions, like the way Dad used to build the tree.

I know there's a poem that says only God can make a tree, but obviously Joyce Kilmer never met my dad.

We would always find the perfect tree at the top of a much taller perfect tree. After we had revived my brother from the fall that invariably occurred when attempting to cut a treetop while being attacked by a mockingbird, we'd bring the tree home and find that it didn't fit into the house. So, Dad would start alterations by cutting the bottom off and then trying to make the tree stand up.

If it had a few bald spots, Dad would get extra branches, pull out that trusty little hole-drilling thing, and punch those branches right into the trunk of that tree.

All the while, Mom would be standing just out of falling range of the tree, supervising and giving moral support. "A little to the left. No, maybe the right. Well, if you're going to put it there, I'm just leaving."

And that moral support would be just about enough to drive Dad to his other tradition—the Christmas bourbon—earlier than usual.

They just don't make traditions like that anymore.

Thursday, December 27

✎ Learning to Play

Stress is simply the cornerstone of my life. For Christmas, my better half tried to help me slow down by giving me gifts like a board game and a fiction book. Other than my romance novels, I have not read anything that was not business-related in the last decade. I started reading it. Then I found myself analyzing the plot, dissecting the characters, and thinking about how I would have written the chapters differently.

So I moved on to the game. I stared at it as though it were a UFO, a kitchen stove, or some other such object that I have never come in contact with.

"What do I do with this?"

"You play it. You know, we sit down and spend a little time just having fun."

"Oh." I contemplated this idea. "What happens then?"

"One of us wins and we're finished."

"I see. Do I learn anything from this?"

"How to relax, maybe."

"Do I make any money if I win?"

"No."

"Will I learn any useful skills?"

He opted for humor. "You could learn how to lose with dignity."

"Yeah, that sounds useful." I grimaced and he could tell I was about to launch into a sarcastic diatribe, so he cut me off.

"Look, it's just for fun." His patience was wearing a little thin.

"So," I tried to assimilate the whole idea of a game. "We sit down. We play this game. Then it's over and we have nothing to show for it except that one of us is a winner at this game. Then we put it in the closet."

"That's right. There's nothing to learn from it. There's no reward. It's just an opportunity to slow down and have a little fun."

I decided that the game could be fun, but before we sat down to play, I insisted on doing something that he's not accustomed to—reading the instructions. I set the game up on the dining room table. Then I left for an hour to formulate my strategy plan on the computer. I went to the kitchen to figure out what snacks would be easiest and neatest to eat while we played the game. I made a list of possible bets that the winner could win from the loser, including dishwashing, litter box cleaning, and coffee duty.

When I came back and told him all the things I had accomplished, I discovered that he had decided to bypass those first few steps of the game, where 1) we sit down, 2) play the game, and 3) win or lose. He put the game in the closet.

✎ Don't Run with Scissors or Your Face Will Stick Like That

"Don't run with scissors! It's impossible to cut straight when you're running." Yes, ever since the days when I was gaining valuable insights like that from my mother, I've continued to learn many important lessons in life. Lessons that are sometimes funny, sometimes hard, and always needed.

And today, to wrap up the year, I am stopping and taking time to compile those lessons into a list so that I don't forget them and have to learn them all over again.

✓ When I start taking myself too seriously, I need to visit my mother. She helps me overcome "big-shot-ism" by telling that story of when I tried to put both legs into one hole of my training pants.

✓ A leap of faith has to include a fall or two. If not, there's no need for the faith.

✓ We were smarter when we were children. When we played, we played. When we worked, like cleaning our rooms, we worked. And then we forgot about that work as soon as we got back out into the yard to play again. And we never once used the term "multi-tasking."

✓ My pets are smarter than me. If not, they would be going to work every day, balancing the checkbook on weekends, and cleaning out the litter box, while I was sitting on the couch scratching myself.

✓ If I were skinny, I'd find something else to obsess about.

✓ If it takes someone else to empower me, then it's not real power.

✓ There are no right or wrong decisions—there are only different choices that can be made. However, if there were such a thing as a wrong decision, giving a guy named Carrot Top a role in a commercial series would have been one of them.

✓ If I take myself seriously, it's easier to be embarrassed.

✓ Knowing the rules doesn't guarantee that everyone is abiding by them. The number of traffic accidents at four-way stops is a great illustration of this.

✓ Hurricanes are nature's way of making me clean unnecessary items off my back porch.

✓ Winning the biggest and most expensive toys is not the most important thing. How much fun is a seesaw without a friend on the other side?

✓ Sometimes in life, it's not the ingredients that determine the outcome. Chicken, sausage, rice, and spices can make jambalaya or they can make a mess. It all depends on how I cook them.

✓ When things don't work out right, the strongest word I can say is, "Next!" And when things work out right, the strongest word I can say is, "Next!"

And so, this year—I took a leap of faith and left a good job behind; I was amazed when I gained thirty pounds, lost them, and then found them again; I cursed like a sailor when a double play ended the Braves season; and I joyfully celebrated my Dad's eighty-ninth birthday and my Mom's thirty-ninth birthday (yeah—you tell her that's mathematically impossible). And, with all those moments behind me, I have only one thing to say:

"Next!"